European Patent Convention

European Patent Convention

Alexandru Cristian Strenc

This book was originally published as a monograph in the International Encyclopaedia of Laws/Intellectual Property Law.

Founding Editor: Roger Blanpain
General Editor: Frank Hendrickx
Volume Editor: Hendrik Vanhees

Wolters Kluwer

Published by:
Kluwer Law International B.V.
PO Box 316
2400 AH Alphen aan den Rijn
The Netherlands
E-mail: international-sales@wolterskluwer.com
Website: lrus.wolterskluwer.com

Sold and distributed in North, Central and South America by:
Wolters Kluwer Legal & Regulatory U.S.
7201 McKinney Circle
Frederick, MD 21704
United States of America
Email: customer.service@wolterskluwer.com

Sold and distributed in all other countries by:
Air Business Subscriptions
Rockwood House
Haywards Heath
West Sussex
RH16 3DH
United Kingdom
Email: international-customerservice@wolterskluwer.com

ISBN 978-94-035-0304-2

e-Book: ISBN 978-94-035-0183-3
web-PDF: ISBN 978-94-035-0251-9

The Author

Alexandru Cristian Strenc was born on 17 December 1949. He graduated from the Polytechnic University of Bucharest, Faculty of Control and Computers in 1972 and received his PhD in Process Control Systems in 1983.

Between 1972 and 1984, he was a researcher in the 'Institute for Design and Research in Control Systems' and from 1984, headed a working team on 'Computer Aided Design' set up in the mentioned institute.

Since 1988, he has worked with the State Office for Inventions and Trademarks as a patent examiner in the field of computer-implemented inventions and served as Deputy Director General and also as Director General from 1990 to 2014.

He is the author of numerous books, articles, and papers in the field of Intellectual Property published in Romania and abroad.

His most relevant books published in Romania are: *Handbook on Patent Law* in two volumes issued in 2005 and 2007, *Information Technology-Protection and Enforcement of Intellectual Property Rights* issued in 2010 and *Capitalization of the Research Results in Universities – Intellectual Property and Business Plan*.

On the international field, Strenc's activity is closely related with Wolters Kluwer, where under his name were issued the monograph 'Intellectual Property Law in Romania' in 2002, 2012, 2016, as well as the monograph 'European Software Directives and European Software Patents' in 2017.

In 2000, 2001, and 2003, he affected stages of studies at the Max Planck Institute for Intellectual Property, the European Patent Office, the US Patent and Trademark Office, the WIPO, the Danish School for Public Administration. In 1997 and 1998 he acted as Vice-President of the General Assembly of WIPO.

Strenc was till 2014, a member of the Administrative Council and Patent Law Committee and of the European Patent Organisation and between 2011 and 2014, Chair of the Supervisory Board of the European Patent Academy.

He also headed the Romanian Delegation in the Administrative Council of the Community Plant Variety Office and the Working Party of Intellectual Property-Patents of the EU Council which negotiated the Unitary Patent Package.

Equally, he headed his delegation at the Diplomatic Conference for the revision of the EPC in November 2000 as well as at the Conferences in Paris in 1999 and respectively in 2000 in London, on translations agreement.

The Author

Strenc was President of the Editorial Board of the Romanian Review of Industrial Property and teaches since 2007 on IP matters at Bucharest Polytechnic University.

Currently, he is a European and national patent attorney and is managing the IP Company – Strenc Solutions for Innovation.

Table of Contents

The Author 3

List of Abbreviations 11

Preface 15

General Introduction 17

§1. European Patent System: A Success and Dynamic Story in a Challenging Patent World 17
I. Success Story 17
A. European Patent Convention 17
B. European Patent Organisation 17
C. European Patent Office 18
II. Dynamic Evolution 19

Chapter 1. Historic Evolution Towards the EPC 1973 20

§1. First Developments Towards European Harmonization in the Field of Patents 20

§2. Relevant International Law 22
I. Strasbourg Convention 1963 on the Unification of Certain Points of Substantive Law on Patents for Invention 22
II. PCT 24

§3. Munich Diplomatic Conference 1973 for the Setting up of a European System for the Grant of Patents 24

§4. Basis of the New Patent System Established by EPC 1973 25

Chapter 2. Main Revision Points Adopted in the Munich Diplomatic Conference of November 2000 27

§1. Preliminaries 27

§2. Developments in International Patent Law 27
I. Harmonization with TRIPS 28

II. Harmonization with PLT 2000 28

§3. NEEDS AND EXPECTATIONS OF THE USER COMMUNITY 30
I. Substantive Patent Law 30
A. Inventions in All Fields of Technology 30
B. Inventions on Medical Methods 31
C. Prior Art Effect of European Patent Applications 32
D. Extent of Protection 32
II. Centralized Limitation Procedure 33
III. Appeal Procedure 34
IV. EURO-PCT Applications: Lack of Unity 34
V. Reducing the Cost of European Patents and Improving Litigation Concerning European Patents 35
VI. Attorney-Client Relationship 35

§4. INTERNAL EPO OWN REQUIREMENTS 36
I. BEST Implementation 36
II. Priority Documents 37

§5. FLEXIBILITY OF THE EPC 37

Chapter 3. Basic Provisions of the Current EPC 40

§1. PRELIMINARIES 40

§2. LEGAL NATURE AND CONTENT 40

§3. GENERAL AND INSTITUTIONAL PROVISIONS 41
I. General Provisions 41
II. The EPOrg 43
A. Status 43
B. Membership 44
C. Institutional Matters 45
III. The EPO 46
A. Premises and Staff 46
1. Further Details 47
B. Responsibility and Task 47
C. Management and Structure 47
D. Languages of the EPO 51
IV. The AC 53
A. Composition and Committees 53
1. Board B28 53
2. Budget and Finance Committee 54
3. Committee on Patent Law 55
4. Technical and Operational Support Committee 55
5. Supervisory Board of the Academy 55
6. Select Committee 56

B. Competence and Procedural Aspects 56
V. Financial Provisions 59

§4. SUBSTANTIVE PATENT LAW 60
I. Patentable Inventions; Inventions Excluded or Excepted from Patentability 60
A. Patentable Inventions 60
1. General provisions 60
2. Patentable Biotechnological Inventions 61
B. Inventions Excluded from Patentability 62
1. Discoveries, Scientific Theories and Mathematical Methods 63
2. Aesthetic Creations 63
3. Schemes, Rules and Methods for Performing Mental Acts, Playing Games or Doing Business, Program of Computers 64
4. Presentations of Information 64
C. Inventions Excepted form Patentability 65
1. Inventions Contrary to Ordre Public or Morality 65
2. Plant or Plant Varieties 66
3. Animals or Animal Varieties 67
4. Medical Methods 67
II. Patentability Conditions 69
A. Novelty 69
1. State of the Art and Absolute Novelty 69
2. Novelty of Medical Uses 70
3. Non-prejudicial Disclosure Versus 'Grace Period' 72
4. Basic Consideration in Assessing Novelty 74
B. Inventive Step 75
1. Problem Solution Approach 75
2. Could-Would Test 76
3. Invention Obvious to a Person Skilled in the Art 77
4. Secondary Indicia of Inventive Step 78
C. Industrial Application 79
III. Persons Entitled to a European Patent 80
IV. Effects of the European Patent and the European Patent Application 82
A. Term of Protection 82
B. Translation of the European Patent 83
C. Effects of a European Patent Application 85
V. Extent of Protection 86
VI. The European Patent Application as an Object of Property 88

§5. GRANT PROCEDURE 89
I. Filing of a European Patent Application 89
II. Conditions Required to a European Patent Application 90
III. Basic Steps in European Patent Grant Procedure 96

A. Examination under Receiving Section and a Search Division 98
B. Substantive Examination 100
C. Accelerated Prosecution Procedure of European Applications 102

§6. Opposition Procedure and Limitation and Revocation Procedures 103
I. Legal Nature 103
II. Grounds of Opposition 105
III. Procedural Steps 105
A. Entitlement to File and Opposition 105
B. Procedure and Decisions 106
C. Accelerated Processing of Oppositions 108

§7. Appeals Procedure 109
I. Legal Nature 109
II. Procedural Steps 110
III. Decisions or Opinions of the Enlarged Board of Appeal 111
IV. Governance of the Boards of Appeal 113

§8. Common Provisions 114
I. Common Provisions on Procedure 114
II. Representation 116

§9. Impact on National Law 119
I. Conversion into a National Patent Application 119
II. Revocation of European Patents 121
III. Prior Rights 121
IV. Other Effects 122

§10. Special Agreements 122
I. Provision on Unitary Patents 123
II. Other Agreements Between the Contracting States 124

§11. International Applications Under the PCT 126

§12. Transitional and Final Provisions 127

Chapter 4. Additional Texts 130

§1. General Considerations 130

§2. Implementing Regulations 130
I. General Aspects 130

§3. Protocol on Recognition 131
I. General Aspects 131
II. Substantive Provisions 131

§4. Protocol on Privileges and Immunities 133
I. General Aspects 133
II. Basic Provisions 133

§5. Protocol on the Centralisation 134
I. General Aspects 134
II. Main Provisions 135

§6. Protocol on the Interpretation of Article 69 of the Convention 136
I. General Aspects 136
II. Basic Provisions 137

§7. Protocol on Staff Complement 139

Chapter 5. Relationship to Other International Conventions 140

§1. General Considerations 140

§2. Relationship with the PCT; the EURO-PCT Approach 140
I. EPC as Regional Patent Treaty Within the Meaning of PCT 141
A. Applicable Law 141
B. EPO Tasks as PCT Authority 142
II. Substantive Harmonization with EPC 143

§3. Relation with the London Agreement 145

§4. Relation with the Unitary Patent System 148
I. Legal Basis 148
II. Select Committee and Secondary Legislation 149
III. Main Characteristics of the Unitary Patent Protection 150
IV. Unified Patent Court 152
A. Jurisdiction and Structure 152
B. Competence 153
C. Sources of Law 154

§5. Relation with the EPLA (Draft) 154

Chapter 6. State of the Play and Predictable Evolution of the EPC 158

§1. Political Developments on the Unitary Patent System and Specifically on the UPC 158

§2. International Developments in the Field of Patents 159

§3. INTERNAL EVOLUTIONS AND NEEDS OF AN IMPROVED PROCEDURE OF THE EPC 161

§4. CHALLENGES TO THE FUTURE 162

Selected Bibliography 165

Index 167

List of Abbreviations

AC	Administrative Council of the EPOrg
B28	Board of Administrative Council of the EPOrg
BEST	Bringing Examination and Search Together (EPO approach on examination procedure)
BFC	Budget and Finance Committee of the AC
BGH	Bundesgerichtshof (Federal Court of Justice-Germany)
BUSINESSEUROPE	Confederation of European Business
CA xx/yy	Document no. xx of the AC of the EPOrg issued in the year yy
CCD	Common Citation Document
CFI	Court of First Instance
CII	Computer-Implemented Invention
CJEU	Court of Justice of the European Union
COO	Chief Operating Officer
D xx/yy	Decision number xx of the year yy of the Disciplinary Board of Appeal
DG x	Directorate-General x of the EPO
EC	European Commission
ECfE	Early Certainty from Examination (EPO project)
ECfO	Early Certainty from Opposition (EPO project)
ECfS	Early Certainty from Search (EPO project)
EEA	European Economic Area
EEC	European Economic Community
EP	European Patent under the EPC
EPC 1973	Convention on the Grant of European Patents of 5.10.1973

List of Abbreviations

EPC 2000	European Patent Convention 2000 as negotiated by the Diplomatic Conference in Munich 2000 and adopted by decision of the Administrative Council of 28.6.2001
EPI	Institute of Professional Representatives before the European Patent Office
EPLA	European Patent Litigation Agreement
EPO	European Patent Office
EPOrg	European Patent Organisation
EU	European Union
EUIPO	European Union Intellectual Property Office
EURO-PCT	Procedures under the PCT before the EPO
G xx/yy	Decision No. xx from the year (last two digits) yy of the Enlarged Board of Appeal of the EPO
ILO	International Labor Organization
IP	Intellectual Property
IPEA	International Preliminary Examination Authority
IPRP	International Preliminary Report on Patentability
IPER	International Preliminary Examination Report
IPR	Intellectual Property Rights
ISA	International Search Authority
IT	Information Technology
ITC	Information Technology Communication
J xx/yy	Decision No. xx from the year (last two digits) yy of the Legal Board of Appeal of the EPO
MR xx/yy	Document no. xx from the year yy of the Diplomatic Conference EPC 2000
MS	Member State of the EU
NPI	Nordic Patent Institute
NPO	National Patent Office
OJ xx/yy	Official Journal of the European Patent Office nr. xx from the year yy
PACE	Programme for accelerated prosecution of EP applications
PCen	Protocol on the Centralisation of the European Patent System
PD	Principal Directorate
PPI	Protocol on Privileges and Immunities of the EPOrg

PR	Protocol on Jurisdiction and the Recognition of Decisions
PCT	Patent Cooperation Treaty
PLC	Patent Law Committee of the AC
PLT	Patent Law Treaty
SIS	Supplementary International Search –under PCT-
SISA	Supplementary International Search Authority–under PCT-
SPLT	Substantive Patent Law Treaty-Draft
T xx/yyyy	Decision No. xx from the year yyyy of the Technical Board of Appeal of the EPO
TFEU	Treaty on the Functioning of the European Union
TOSC	Technical and Operational Support Committee of the EPOrg
TRIPS	Trade-Related Aspects of Intellectual Property
UDEC	User Driven Early Certainty (EPO proposal for a possibility to postpone the start of the substantive examination)
UPC	Unified Patent Court
UPCtA	Agreement on a Unified Patent Court
UPP	Unitary Patent Protection (European patent with unitary effect)
VP	Vice-Presidents of the EPO
WIPO	World Intellectual Property Organization
WTO	World Trade Organization
XML	Extensible Markup Language

List of Abbreviations

Preface

By the nature of my duties, I interfaced with a couple of international conventions and related institutions and organizations in the field of Intellectual Property.

Among them, the European Patent Convention (EPC) and its coordinating and implementing bodies, the European Patent Organisation (EPOrg) and the European Patent Office (EPO), are particularly close and quite dear to me.

This feeling comes indeed from my direct and – if I am allowed to say – sometimes significant involvement and participation in many administrative, technical, and legal matters and activities connected with them.

It is a challenging story which starts from representing the Patent Office of my country – Romania – for many years in the Administrative Council and in the Patent Law Committee of the EPOrg. The same happened in the Diplomatic Conference of Munich (2000) for the revision of the EPC and in the Intergovernmental Conferences of Paris (1998) and London (1999) and continues with chairing the Supervisory Board of the European Patent Academy for a number of years.

I also represented, for the whole relevant period, my country in the Brussels negotiations for the conclusion of the Unitary Patent system, which originates in the substance of the EPC.

It is therefore probably one of the most exciting corollaries of this activity, to have the opportunity, given by KLUWER, to draft and to express in this monograph, a lively experience. With all my humble pride, I can say that it comes not only from many direct contributory participations and experiences received from the inside of the various forums of the European patent system but also from many hours of deep study which enabled me to prove a certain level of representation.

From the very beginning, I was aware of possible important expectations arising from this direct experience.

But not a hint of concern came from the inner difficulty of concentrating the vast content of the whole EPC itself in the relatively small size of the written material allowed under this series.

I was really compelled to remain within a certain procedural plan in my effort to present the core and the essence of the EPC.in the monograph.

First of all, my presentation follows, in general lines, the structure of the EPC but does not necessarily discuss each and every article.

Second, I restricted to what I considered necessary regarding detailed implementing aspects of the EPC as well as the doctrinaire opinions. My focus was rather addressed to the patentability and patenting procedure as being the core business of the EPC and EPO, and on the jurisprudence given by the EPO case law, starting from the presumption that it clarifies, in the most adequate way, the substance of the European patent system as directly originating from it.

Third, whenever the situation offered the possibility, I tried to escape from a rigid analysis of some of the EPC provisions by presenting something from the life, current structure and projects of the EPOrg and EPO.

It only remains for me to hope that the readers will find that I have at least partially met their expectations by mixing all these endeavours in a useful and creative manner.

Last but not least, I am most deeply grateful to distinguished Professor Dr Vanhees, who not only proposed me to write but, as always in the past, encouraged, guided, and supported me in drafting this monograph.

General Introduction

§1. European Patent System: A Success and Dynamic Story in a Challenging Patent World

I. Success Story

A. *European Patent Convention*

1. Among possible parameters that might characterize the historic success of the European Patent Convention (EPC), two are of a particular and indisputable relevance.

2. The first one, for which the grandfathers of the EPC deserve all our respect, is the incredible actuality of the originally negotiated, drafted and agreed text of the EPC 1973.

3. Without forgetting that which have been brought by the Diplomatic Conference of Munich 2000 or by various Decisions of the Administrative Council, a series amendments to the original text, it is also true that the substance of the EPC is equally valid today as was more than forty years ago.

4. The amendments – that will be later analysed – were necessary in order to respond to historical endogen and exogen factors which objectively imposed them. They succeeded indeed in improving many concepts and patenting procedures but in fact, they didn't change them in substance which makes it really impressive.

5. The second factor is the open doors left in the EPC to future developments and the best example is the Unitary Patent system, which has the chance to start next in the future of Europe. If the European countries will take this chance is another story for which the question still remains for the future.

B. *European Patent Organisation*

6. If when founded, the EPOrg started with seven Contracting States (sixteen states signed the EPC 1973) – the organization has today (April 2018), thirty-eight Contracting States.

7. A historical and significant moment for the EPOrg was between 2002 and 2003 when a massive group of central-eastern European countries joined the organization.

8. Without being officially mentioned as such, it represented indeed a certain political crossing of the 'iron curtain' for the European patent system.

9. Note that currently, the European patent protection may be also requested for another two 'extension states' which, although are not Contracting States to the EPC, have instead signed and enforced 'extension agreements'. Representatives of these states have the status of observer in the Administrative Council of the EPOrg (AC).

10. Since 2010, further agreements called 'validation agreements' have been concluded providing for European patents to have effect in Non-contracting States. These 'validation agreements' are not limited to European countries.

C. European Patent Office

11. A simple comparison between the figures shown by the number of European patent applications processed by the European Patent Office (EPO) during its time is eloquent in itself for the success of the European patent system.

12. First-year activity of the 'small baby' EPO reports[1] approximately 3,600 European patent applications filed which together with the Patent Cooperation Treaty (PCT) applications raised the total number of 4,011 applications

13. Only three years later, the situation was the following:[2] 'from January to the end of July 1981, over 12,600 European applications were received and around 1350 EURO-PCT filings which was likely to result in some 23000 or 24000 filings by the end of the year'. This amount was processed by approximately 533 search examiners and 204 substantive examiners.

14. Since then, a substantial and even dramatic increase in the number of patent applications was reported from approx. 60,000 in the year 1995, 100,000 in 2000, 134,000 in 2009 and over 165,000 in 2017.

1. Griset Pascal- The European Patent A European Success Story for Innovation; pg. 1126; Käsel Buch 2013.
2. Griset Pascal- The European Patent A European Success Story for Innovation; pg. 147; Käsel Buch 2013.

15. This evolution led to a situation where the EPO become the second-largest intergovernmental organization in Europe, employing currently a staff[3] of approximately 6,800 persons from over thirty countries, of which, approximately 4,300 being patent examiners and approximately 140 members of the Boards of Appeal.

16. The EPO is also the largest PCT International Searching Authority (ISA).

17. The facts speak for themselves and probably nothing could be added in this respect.

II. Dynamic Evolution

18. Since 1973, the EPC, as a whole, proved to be the subject matter of a dynamic evolution due to revisions and amendments which led to the version in force today.

19. In fact, the EPC in force and which is, in fact, the object of our analysis is the text of the EPC of 5 October 1973 as revised by the Act revising Article 63 EPC of 17 December 1991 and the Act revising the EPC of 29 November 2000.

20. As an integral part of the EPC, the text in the Implementing Regulations is that of the EPC of 5 October 1973 as adopted by decision of the AC on 7 December 2006 and as last amended by decision of the AC on 14 October 2015.

21. A significant part of this dynamic evolution which will be subsequently presented relates to the negotiations held and the European Union (EU) Regulations adopted together with other relevant secondary law on the Unitary Patent system, entirely based on relevant provisions within the EPC.

22. As being the subject of an ongoing process, this dynamic evolution really has the chance to expand and develop in the near future.

3. EPO- Social Report for the year 2016; pg. 8–9.

Chapter 1. Historic Evolution Towards the EPC 1973

§1. First Developments Towards European Harmonization in the Field of Patents

23. The history of the European patent system started after the end of the Second World War and mankind in general – (western) Europeans in particular – considered the ways and means to rebuild the basis of a broken cooperation, in which Intellectual Property (IP) in general and patents in particular, played an important role.

24. While international agreements were being made with respect to patent law, Europe was developing its own agreements exclusively among European nations

25. The very first real European initiative to be implemented in the field of patents was the setting up of the International Patent Institute (IIB) in 1947 under an agreement concluded by the Benelux countries: Netherlands, Belgium, Luxembourg, and respectively France, which entered into force in 1949.

26. The IIB headquarter was established in Den Hague and the Institute's main task to carry out novelty searches on the patent applications originating from its Member States.

27. At various moments of time, other European countries: Italy, Monaco, Switzerland, Turkey and last, the UK, joined the Institute. It is extremely relevant and not at all a surprise – the reasons for which will be given in Chapter 2 §4 I, that the IIB ceased to exist as an independent legal entity,[4] once the EPO started to function in 1978 and practically, the IIB merged with the other structural entities of the EPO but formed the basis of the EPO's search activity in its headquarter from Den Hague.

28. The year 1949 is equally important for the history of the EPC[5] because in September 1949, the Council of Europe, by the significant voice of the French Senator Henri Longchambon, expressed the necessity for setting up an EPO within the so-called *Longchambon plan*. The Council of Europe provided indeed a forum for discussion which would lead to the further internationalization of European patent laws. It marked the starting point of a European patent law aimed at a 'European patent' to be granted by an EPO.

29. His (probably too) visionary plan of that historic moment was not agreed as such by the council's Committee of Experts in patent matters which would eventually start its activity in 1951 in Strasbourg.

---

4. Lise Dybdhal- European Patents; pg. 6, Heymans, 2001.
5. Griset Pascal- The European Patent A European Success Story for Innovation; pg. 45–53; Käsel Buch 2013.

30. The meetings of the committee nevertheless led to two conventions.

31. The first one, on the formalities required for patent applications,[6] aimed at establishing a set of maximal formal conditions for patent applications to be considered by the Member States in their national patent law.

32. The convention, to which adhered twenty Member States, was ultimately a success but subsequent developments on the PCT and EPC, made it superfluous.

33. The second one, the convention on the International Patent Classification (IPC),[7] which was ratified by fifteen states and latter was brought under the umbrella of World Intellectual Property Organization (WIPO), developed towards the legal basis of the agreement concerning the IPC from Strasbourg, 1971.

34. The council's committee continued its work on substantive patent law, resulting in the signature of the Strasbourg Patent Convention in 1963,[8] which is largely presented in §2, I and which constituted a real basis for the harmonization of European patent laws. In this respect, it should be remembered that 'it formed the basis for the substantive provisions of Art. 52 to 74 EPC'.[9]

35. It was apparently clear that the diversity of patent laws posed a serious threat to the functioning of a single European market and thus was evocated the possibility of a unified patent system of some sort, synergic to the newborn economic and political system. By 1959, the possibility of a separate patent system alongside national systems emerged and began the move towards a European Commission (EC) patent, but for pragmatic reasons, the project had split into two and comprised moves towards, on the one hand, a system for members and non-members of the EU and on the other hand a unitary system primarily aimed at EU members.[10]

36. The first EPC was drafted in 1962 where it clearly expressed the approach towards European patents coexisting with national patents and having an autonomous and unitary status. This basic idea was in line with the orientation of interested circles but for political reasons, the activity of the working party on patents stopped for next four years.

---

6. European Convention relating to the formalities required for patent applications; Paris, 11 XII. 1953; Council of Europe European Treaty Series No. 16.
7. European Convention on the international classification of patents for invention; Paris, 19.XII.1954-Council of Europe European Treaty Series No. 17.
8. Convention on the Unification of Certain Points of Substantive Law on Patents for Invention Strasbourg 1963 European Treaty Series No. 47.
9. Lise Dybdhal- European Patents; pg. 7, Heymans, 2001.
10. Robert Pitkethly-The European Patent System: Implementing Patent Law Harmonisation- paper originally presented in OHP format at the International Symposium on Innovation and Patents held at The Institute of Innovation Research of Hitotsubashi University, Japan on 12–13 Feb. 1999.

§2. RELEVANT INTERNATIONAL LAW

I. Strasbourg Convention 1963 on the Unification of Certain Points of Substantive Law on Patents for Invention

37. This convention, signed in Strasbourg on 27 November 1963, declared from the very beginning in preamble, to be within the spirit of the Council of Europe in order 'to achieve a greater unity between its members for the purpose, among others, of facilitating their economic and social progress by agreements and common action in economic, social, cultural, scientific, legal and administrative matters'.

38. The key purpose of this convention was to unify both procedural and substantive requirements of the patent system throughout Europe, thereby encouraging industry and invention in all of Europe.

39. It is impressive to find out that the substantive patentability concepts and conditions provided for in the future EPC have been really based on the text of the convention.

40. Thus, Article 1, in almost exactly same wording as the EPC on the three patentability conditions of inventions, (Chapter 4 II) provides that 'patents shall be granted for any inventions which are susceptible of industrial application, which are new and which involve an inventive step'.

41. Article 2 of the Strasbourg Convention can be easily recognized in the substance of the EPC provisions on 'exceptions to patentability' (*see* Chapter 3 §4 I *C*) when it stipulates that:

> The Contracting States shall not be bound to provide for the grant of patents in respect of inventions the publication or exploitation of which would be contrary to ordre public or morality, provided that the exploitation shall not be deemed to be so contrary merely because it is prohibited by a law or regulation and for plant or animal varieties or essentially biological processes for the production of plants or animals; this provision does not apply to microbiological processes and the products thereof.

42. This can be easily explained by the still large and yet unsolved debate of the time on that topic, why the third exception provided in EPC on medical methods was not considered under the Strasburg Convention.

43. Another remarkable key point in our analysis refers to the three patentability conditions which are practically identically defined in the two conventions.

44. Thus, Article 3 on industrial applicability provides that:

> an invention shall be considered as susceptible of industrial application if it can be made or used in any kind of industry including agriculture

where the later EPC drafting can be easily recognized.

45. The first three paragraphs of Article 4 on novelty stipulating that:

> an invention shall be considered to be new if it does not form part of the state of the art. Subject to the provisions of paragraph 4 of this article, the state of the art shall be held to comprise everything made available to the public by means of a written or oral description, by use, or in any other way, before the date of the patent application or of a foreign application, the priority of which is validly claimed. Any Contracting State may consider the contents of applications for patents made, or of patents granted, in that State, which have been officially published on or after the date referred to in paragraph 2 of this article, as comprised in the state of the art, to the extent to which such contents have an earlier priority date

are similar to the relevant Article in the EPC.

46. The same deep similarity in the inspirational provision of the Strasbourg Convention is found in the text on non-prejudicial disclosure based on the fact that the invention was made public, within six months preceding the filing of the application, if the disclosure was due to, or in consequence of an evident abuse in relation to the applicant or his legal predecessor, or the fact that the applicant or his legal predecessor has displayed the invention at an official, or officially recognized international exhibition.

47. Basis of the inventive step is provided in Article 5 'an invention shall be considered as involving an inventive step if it is not obvious having regard to the state of the art', which will be completed later on in the future EPC with the reference to the 'person skilled in the art' who normally analyses the obviousness of an invention in order to obtain the current drafting of this condition.

48. Another exceptionally important provision for the future text of the EPC on a mixture of concepts regarding the patent application, the disclosure of the invention, and respectively the extent of protection is that of Article 8 providing that:

- The patent application shall contain a description of the invention with the necessary drawings referred to therein and one or more claims defining the protection applied for.
- The description must disclose the invention in a manner sufficiently clear and complete for it to be carried out by a person skilled in the art.
- The extent of the protection conferred by the patent shall be determined by the terms of the claims. Nevertheless, the description and drawings shall be used to interpret the claims.

49. The visionary spirit of this convention, not only for the EPC but also for the future endeavours on community and unitary patent, might be found in Article 7 which provides that ‘ any group of Contracting States who provide for a common patent application may be regarded as a single State … .’ for the purposes of relevant substantive provisions.

50. Procedural requirements including requirements for filing date of the patent application as well as for later procedural steps in defining and examining patentability conditions were adopted in this convention, eventually adopted in the PCT, and later adopted with minimal changes in the EPC.

II. PCT

51. The PCT was signed on 19 June 1970, in Washington, as a result of long negotiations held within the auspices of the WIPO. Although the current European patent system is formally and legally independent from the PCT, the PCT is relevant for our analysis by a direct and clear indication on how the European system interacts with the rest of the world.

52. This interaction will be left for more detail in Chapter 5 §2, but starting from the presumption that the PCT has been concluded almost three years before the EPC seems to naturally consider that the intense discussions and negotiations held under the world forum put their fingertips on the later decided text of the EPC 1973.

53. Nevertheless, historical developments of the negotiations for the PCT[11] indicated in relevant documents that important substantive provisions of the PCT were supported by harmonized European positions already aggregated in the internal negotiations carried under the EPC developments.

54. In line with this assertion, it should be underlined that the real effective history of the EPC 1973 started[12] within the preparatory work of the PCT negotiations where initiative had been taken at European level to call for an intergovernmental conference of the European Economic Community (EEC) states which convened in Luxembourg. Between 1969 and 1972 the conference held a series of sessions which led to the text submitted in Munich Diplomatic Conference.

§3. Munich Diplomatic Conference 1973 for the Setting up of a European System for the Grant of Patents

55. The Diplomatic Conference held its meeting in Munich from 10 September to 6 October 1973 and after long debates, the final text was signed by sixteen states.

56. Twenty-two European states were invited including Yugoslavia and Turkey

11. WIPO- Records of the Washington Diplomatic Conference of the Patent Cooperation Treaty; www.wipo.int/export/sites/www/pct/en/texts/pdf/washington_p171_to_538.pdf
12. Lise Dybdhal- European Patents; pg. 8, Heymans, 2001.

57. It is remarkable as time has shown and proved that the profound and solid basis established in 1973 of the European patent system has remained unchanged in substance, the subsequent amendments (*see* Chapter 2) being rather a matter of improving the functioning of the system than changing it.

58. An Interim Committee with seven working parties was set up by the conference, having the main task of entering into force the convention and the functioning of its executive body, the EPO.

59. A true hard-working activity[13] materialized in the 165 meetings held during over 450 working days which produced 1,450 documents and made it possible for the EPC to enter into force on 7 October 1977 and the EPO itself to open its doors on 1 November 1977. This new patent system was effectively born and from 1 July 1978 started filing European patent applications.

60. The convention was entered into force on 7 October 1977 for the initial following countries: Belgium, Germany (then West Germany), France, Luxembourg, Netherlands, Switzerland and UK, and on 1 May 1978 for Sweden. However, the first patent applications were filed on 1 June 1978

§4. Basis of the New Patent System Established by EPC 1973

61. The EPC 1973 has established[14] a single European procedure for the grant of patents on the basis of a single application and created a uniform body of substantive patent law designed to provide easier, cheaper and stronger protection for inventions in the Contracting States. This procedure is performed by the EPO in one of its three official languages.

62. At the end of the patent application procedure, the EPO grants a single European patent covering all designated states. After grant, the European patent must be validated generally within three months of grant in each state in which the owner intends to enforce its rights. For any states in which the national phase is not validated, protection lapses in that state after grant.

63. The European patent granted and validated for designated states transforms accordingly in a 'bundle' of national patents enforced by national laws of the contracting states.

64. Once granted, the European patent is open to opposition from third parties for a period of nine months.

65. Renewal fees must also be paid in each national state for as long as the individual national phase patents are to remain in force.

---

13. Lise Dybdhal- European Patents; pg. 9, Heymans, 2001.
14. EPO-Guide for applicants: How to get a European patent; A II. 5; July 2017 17th edition.

66. In each Contracting State designated in the patent application, this application and the related European patent granted gives its applicants and later on its proprietor the same rights as would be conferred by a national patent application or the related national patent granted in that state.

67. A published European patent application provides a provisional protection identical in substance with that of which is conferred by national patent law of a Contracting State and which must at least include the right to reasonable compensation in the event of wrongful infringement.

68. The granting procedure performed by a single (European) Patent Office and validity of a European patent is to be assessed in accordance with a uniform body of substantive patent law with which the patent law of the Contracting States has been extensively harmonized.

Chapter 2. Main Revision Points Adopted in the Munich Diplomatic Conference of November 2000

§1. Preliminaries

69. EPC 2000 is the result[15] of a comprehensive revision of EPC 1973 agreed at a Diplomatic Conference in November 2000. It represents the first major revision of the EPC and came into force on 13 December 2007.

70. In 1998, the AC agreed on a comprehensive list of legal and technical points for revision[16] which stayed as the basis of the latter decisions in 2000 and which will be developed in our presentation:

- recent developments in international law, in particular, the TRIPS Agreement and the Patent Law Treaty (PLT) 2000;
- justified needs and expectations of the user community, among others, by establishing a new centralized limitation procedure before the EPO and making possible a limited judicial review of Boards of Appeal decisions;
- meeting the EPO's own demands in view of the workload, *inter alia* by enabling the EPO to introduce the BEST (Bringing Search and Examination Together) system office-wide.
- flexibility of the EPC by deregulation and supplementary powers of decisions to the AC in regulating substantive procedural and legal matters of the EPC;
- increasing adaptability by streamlining the articles of the EPC itself, transferring many details of a procedural or administrative character to the Implementing Regulations.

§2. Developments in International Patent Law

71. Although EPC 1973 proved from the very beginning to have implemented a solid and consistent patent system, the negotiations and conclusions at international level of some major agreements nevertheless seriously addressed the problems and aligned the EPC with existing treaties relating to IP, in particular, the TRIPS and the PLT 2000, and thus afforded further benefits for users of the European patent system in a better and harmonized environment at an international level.

15. Andrew May- Patents in Europe 2008; Effects of the EPC 2000; A Supplement of the Intellectual Asset Management Magazine;April 2008.
16. EPO- Diplomatic Conference for the Revision of the EPC; https://www.epo.org/law-practice/legal-texts/epc/archive/documentation/diplomatic-conference.html.

I. Harmonization with TRIPS

72. Article 53(a) of EPC 1973 provided exclusion from patentability of inventions the *publication* of which would be contrary to 'ordre public' or morality, different from provision of Article 27(2) of the TRIPS Agreement that only excluded from patentability inventions, the *exploitation* of which would be contrary to 'ordre public' or morality. The replacement of the aforementioned concept has been considered as desirable by amending and bringing Article 53(a) in line with the TRIPS and thus, possible different interpretations of exclusion from patentability have been avoided at European and international level.

73. However, it has been considered[17] 'that this clause has had no practical significance so far'.

74. The priority requirements have also been brought in line in accordance with TRIPS so that priority will be recognized from any state which is a member of the World Trade Organization (WTO) instead of filings in Member States of the Paris Convention provided in EPC 1973.

75. This provision extends the geographical area of recognition of priority for instance, to members of economic importance like Chinese Taipei and Hong Kong, China.

76. Further, a priority claim may be made or corrected within sixteen months from the priority date. Further, a translation of the priority document will be requested only if relevant to patentability.

77. Another harmonization point with TRIPS, which will be only mentioned here but which for obvious reason will be developed under Chapter 3 §4 I A, is the alignment of Article 52.1 – Patentable inventions with Article 27.1 TRIPS, by providing that European patents will be granted for all inventions belonging to '*all fields of technology* ...'

II. Harmonization with PLT 2000

78. Under EPC 1973, filing date was subject to condition that the European patent application be filed in one of the EPO's official language and includes a description of the invention and at least one claim in line with the extremely permissive provisions of the PLT regarding the minimum requirements for the accordance of a filing date, accordingly, EPC 2000 brought in its turn, a significant relaxation of these conditions.

17. EPO –CA/16/98 from 18.02.1998.

79. Thus, Article 14 EPC was amended to provide that the application must be filed in one of the EPO's official languages (English, German or French), or, if the application has been filed in another language, be translated in a limited period of time, into one of the official languages.

80. Consequently, under the revised EPC 2000, it is possible to file a European patent application in any language, subject to a subsequent translation into one of the official languages of the EPO must still be provided within two months of filing.

81. On filing requirements,[18] according to the amendments, a mere reference to a previously filed application can take the place of the description and any drawings and there is no requirement to file at least one claim in order to be accorded a filing date. If such a reference is relied upon, then a certified copy of the previously filed application and if necessary, a translation into an official language of the EPO must be filed within two months.

82. The reference made to a previous application is possible based on the fact that the content of the European application is determined by the content of the previously filed application, but it should not be a current and encouraged practice because, in principle, previous applications are drafted according to the patent law of other countries and not for the EPC system.

83. However, this should be considered as a formal requirement and an initial deadline for filing such a translation because if this requirement is not complied with, EPO must issue an invitation to correct the deficiency within a further two-month period. Consequently, from a practical point of view, the applicant is disposed of a minimum of four months to file the translation from the date of filing the application.

84. The requirements for a filing date provided in Article 80 EPC 1973 were transferred to the Implementing Regulations and reflect entirely the substance of Article 5 PLT.

85. In order to implement the PLT 2000, the specific exclusion regarding reinstatement in relation to the timely claiming of priority has been removed.

86. There is a new provision provided in which the loss of a priority right because of failure to file an application within the usual twelve month priority period can be remedied by requesting re-establishment of rights. This has to be done within two months from the date of the loss of the priority right, i.e., two months after the end of the twelve-month period. This applies to new applications and also to existing applications where the two-month term had not yet expired on the date of entry into force.

18. Dehns EPC 2000: Revision of the European Patent Convention; 2010.

87. Subject to the condition that legal conditions for re-establishment have been met, rights are re-established in cases where, in spite of all due care required by the circumstances having been taken, the applicant was unable to observe a time limit. Indeed, the applicants should continue to file at the EPO within twelve months of their first filing, and seek to rely on possible re-establishment of rights only for unexpected situations.

§3. Needs and Expectations of the User Community

I. Substantive Patent Law

A. Inventions in All Fields of Technology

88. As previously mentioned, Article 52 (1) EPC 2000, was brought in line with TRIPS by specifying that '*inventions in all fields of technology*' may be the subject matter of the granted European patents.

89. This new reference point is in line with the European practice of patenting and it strengthened, from a legal perspective, the fact that the protection under the EPC is available for technical inventions of all kinds.

90. However, it should be noted that although without conclusion, long and 'hot' debates took place during the Diplomatic Conference on a possible deletion of computer programs from the list of non-patentable inventions in Article 52(2) (c) in connection with the amended reference to technological inventions.

91. In the *first draft* of the Basic Proposal,[19] it was stated that 'in any event, the deletion of computer programs from Article 52 (2) (c) EPC has met with broad consensus'.

92. At a later stage, the final version of the Basic Proposal[20] indicated a more concessive position by stating that 'the committee on patent law and the Administrative Council have advocated the deletion of programs for computers from Article 52 (2) (c) EPC'. The Basic Proposal stipulated that the deletion of computer programs was *not* intended for broadening the scope of patentable subject matter, but rather that it should merely reflect the current jurisprudence of the EPO's Boards of Appeal.

93. Nevertheless, it has been proposed at the Diplomatic Conference and supported by a large majority of the Member States to abandon the deletion of computer programs and the explanation for this incoherent position with the previously expressed one resulted in the strong opposition against software patents by a number of software developers. In fact, the new coordinated position of the EC Member

19. EPO- CA/100/00.
20. EPO- MR/2/00.

States on maintaining computer programs among the list of non-patentable inventions was defined during a meeting in Brussels on 17 November 2000, that is, three days before the Diplomatic Conference.

B. Inventions on Medical Methods

94. Other significant amendments[21] with regard to patentable inventions covered the sensitive problem of inventions on 'medical methods',

95. Thus, the former provision on exclusion of methods of treatments and diagnostic methods in Article 52 (4) EPC has been moved to a new paragraph (c) with two exceptions to patentability which appear in Article 53 (a) and (b) EPC. The reason for these amendments expressed by a unanimous point of view was that these methods should be excluded from patentability in large primarily in the interest of public health and not, as previously considered, as lacking industrial applicability.

96. Besides this, specific protections in the medical field has been strengthened by legally adding to the existing protection of the so-called first medical use format for known substances and compositions in Article 54(4) EPC, the new text of Article 54(5) dedicated to the protection of the 'second medical use', of substances already used in treatment methods for a second and further therapeutic indications.

97. The prior law allowed use-limited product claims directed to the first medical use of known substances or compositions. This type of protection remained unchanged under the new law but the legal basis for use-limited product claims for specific further medical use was introduced for the first time.

98. Under Article 54(5) EPC 2000, claims directed to compound X for use in a specified second or further medical use was legally allowed, provided the specified new use is both novel and inventive.

99. The new wording of Article 54 EPC 2000 brought in line the legal text with the EPO patenting practice which followed primarily the case law of the Boards of Appeal[22] which allowed *claims* for the first medical use, i.e., for a *general therapeutic purpose*, e.g., as a 'pharmaceutical substance', even if *only a specific use* of the substance is disclosed in the application. The Enlarged Board of Appeal decided that any *further* medical use could receive patent protection under the EPC in spite of the wording of the previous Article 54 which seemed to limit patentability to the *first* medical use. The Enlarged Board allowed the so-called Swiss-type claim, that is, a claim 'directed to the use of a substance or composition for the manufacture of a medicament *for a specific new and inventive therapeutic application*'.[23]

---

21. EPO CA/100/00 e; Basic Proposal for the Revision of the European Patent Convention.
22. T 128/ 82, 'Pyrrolidine derivatives/ Hoffmann-La-Roche', OJ 1984.
23. G 5/ 83, 'Second medical indication/ EISAI', OJ 1985.

C. Prior Art Effect of European Patent Applications

100. In line with all main patent laws, EPC provides that the contents of European patent applications having an earlier filing or as the case might be, an earlier priority date, published after the relevant date of a later application are prior art for the assessment of novelty but not for that of inventive step. EPC 1973 had nevertheless a limitation which produced problems of implementation when stipulating that the earlier application was only prior art for designated states designated in both applications in question and for which the designation fees have been validly paid for the earlier application. In the new wording of Article 54(3) the revised EPC 2000 stipulates that the earlier application will be prior art for all Contracting States regardless of which states are currently designated in the earlier case, which will normally eliminate the situation of interpreting different claim versions for different Contracting States in assessing novelty.

101. In the same line of effect on the prior art, the EPO could invite the applicant to provide the reference numbers of national patent applications on the invention to which a given European patent application is related. Within the EPC 2000, the EPO is given the greater competence to invite the applicant to provide information on prior art taken into consideration in patent proceedings elsewhere concerning the invention and thus, the EPO may request information about prior art cited against corresponding applications.

102. Failure to supply the requested information may result in the situation where the concerned application will be deemed to be withdrawn.

D. Extent of Protection

103. EPC 2000 introduced the new Article 2 of the Protocol on Interpretation of Article 69 relating to the extent of protection conferred by a European patent, according to which ' due account shall be taken of any element which is equivalent to an element specified in the claims'.

104. Remarkably, the initial proposal of the EPO was to introduce not only this reference from Article 2 to the 'due account' accorded to an equivalent element specified in the claims, but to have also a definition of an 'equivalent element' and even more, to provide[24] that the scope of protection conferred by a patent should be construed in the light of statements made during prosecution history.

105. Strong opposition expressed by most of the EPC Member States during Diplomatic Conference lead to a 'rejection solution' of these two provisions, the conclusion being that definition of an equivalent element and possibility to interpret

24. Nicholas Fox- A Guide to the EPC 2000, pg. 45, CIPA 2007.

claims in the light of 'prosecution history' should be left at the interpretation of national courts which [25] 'might apply the doctrine of equivalence in a flexible and "fair" way'.

II. Centralized Limitation Procedure

106. The EPC 1973, provided outside of opposition proceedings, no centralized mechanism for amending European patents post-grant, and consequently, amendments – where necessary – could be performed only on national legal bases in each Contracting State. The EPC 2000 introduced for the first time a centralized mechanism for requesting amendment of a patent post-grant at the EPO, with effect in all EPC Member States in which the patent was validated, which significantly simplifies the procedures, and reduces the cost, of amending a granted European patent, where necessary.

107. The new Article 105a provides that a patent proprietor may request that the scope of protection of his patent be limited by an amendment of the claims, or that the patent be revoked completely. The request can be filed at any time, but care should be taken to avoid adding subject matter with the limitation and to ensure that the other requirements of the EPC are fulfilled.

108. Accepted limitations or revocations will have effect backdated to the date of grant of the patent. The EPO will examine[26] whether the requirements for limitation or revocation of the European patent are met but will not examine the amended claims for novelty or inventive step. The request can be filed at any time, but must not be added subject matter with the limitation and other requirements of the EPC being fulfilled.

109. The procedure is not open to opposition by third parties and there is no restricted number of times a single patent may be amended using this procedure.

110. If an opposition is filed, then the EPO will terminate any limitation proceedings already commenced by the patent proprietor, and if any request for limitation or revocation is filed when opposition proceedings are pending, then the request is deemed not to have been filed.

111. While opposition proceedings are pending, a request for revocation or limitation cannot validly be filed. If at the time of filing an opposition to a European patent, limitation proceedings in respect of that patent are pending, the Examining Division shall terminate the limitation proceedings and order the reimbursement of the limitation fee.

25. EPO CA/100/00 e; Basic Proposal for the Revision of the European Patent Convention.
26. EPO CA/100/00 e; Basic Proposal for the Revision of the European Patent Convention.

112. Central limitation proceedings do not take precedence over national proceedings if the latter were filed earlier, but a limitation resulting from national proceedings may be extended to further Contracting States of the EPC by means of those limitation proceedings.

III. Appeal Procedure

113. The EPC 2000 introduced for the first time the review of decisions of a Board of Appeal, this appears to be only a first step to perhaps subsequently allowing for a complete review of Board of Appeal decisions, because a petition for review by the Enlarged Board of Appeal may be filed only where a fundamental procedural defect occurred in appeal proceedings or where a criminal act may have influenced the decision.

IV. EURO-PCT Applications: Lack of Unity

114. Within EPC 1973, if lack of unity was found by the EPO acting as an ISA during the international search and no additional international search fees were paid, the EPO would issue an invitation in the regional phase to pay further search fees and have additional inventions searched.

115. Similarly, if a supplementary search was carried out by the EPO in the regional phase, subject to the condition that the international search report was drawn up by an ISA other than the EPO, and lack of unity was then found, the applicant was given the opportunity to have additional inventions searched. Examination in the regional phase could then be based on any of the inventions for which search fees had been paid.

116. Under the EPC 2000,[27] if the EPO was the ISA, it can only examine an invention in the regional phase which it searched during the international phase. If the international search report is being drawn up by the EPO and non-unity is found, it should be considered carefully whether further search fees deserve to be paid for inventions of interest since there is no opportunity to pay further search fees in the regional phase and non-searched inventions can only be pursued via divisional applications.

117. Furthermore, under the EPC 2000, any supplementary European search is carried out only on the first invention mentioned in the claims regardless of whether or not lack of unity was found during the international search. The EPO examines only this invention and therefore the invention of greatest interest should be presented first in the claims used for EPO regional phase entry so that it is searched accordingly.

---

27. Dehns EPC 2000: Revision of the European Patent Convention; 2010.

V. Reducing the Cost of European Patents and Improving Litigation Concerning European Patents

118. The amendments brought by the Munich Conference 2000 to the older Part IX *Special Agreements* made it an exceptionally important tool for the future developments of the EPC. Thus, to the existent provisions on unitary patents which led to the future Unitary Patent system (*see* Chapter 3 §10 I) has been introduced a new Article 149a EPC, which will be commented there and is meant to create a clear legal basis for future agreements between the EPC Contracting States concerning on matters as translation requirements (*see* London Agreement in Chapter 5 §2) or litigation concerning European patents (*see* European Patent Litigation Agreement (EPLA) in Chapter 5 §4).

119. Let us recall that the Paris Intergovernmental Conference of 1999 had mandated two working parties on 'Cost Reduction' and respectively on 'Litigation', to submit to the governments of the EPC Contracting States and to the EPC Revision Conference proposals aiming at reducing the cost of European patents and improving litigation concerning European patents.[28] The mandate included the task of drawing up optional protocols to the EPC with a view to limit translation requirements and to create an integrated judicial system and has been successfully accomplished in the period following the Munich Diplomatic Conference.

120. Thus, the new Article 149a offered a clear legal basis in the EPC for enacting London Agreement and EPLA and their interface with EPC and EPO, considered as special agreements within the meaning of the EPC.

VI. Attorney-Client Relationship

121. EPC 2000 added a new subparagraph (d) to the older Article 134a. according to which 'the obligation of confidentiality of the professional representative and the privilege from disclosure in proceedings before the European Patent Office in respect of communications between a professional representative and his client or any other person' falls under the AC's competency to adopt and amend provisions governing this issue.

122. Following this line, Article 2 of the Regulation on Discipline for professional representatives adopted by the AC provides that secrecy relating to confidential information must be maintained by the professional representative.

123. The presumption was that it appeared[29] 'necessary to introduce a representative-client privilege applicable in EPO proceedings, equivalent to that

28. EPO OJ1999, 545ff.
29. EPO CA/100/00 e; Basic Proposal for the Revision of The European Patent Convention.

existing in the US with a view to protecting – in the course of US proceedings – the confidence of communications between European professional representatives and their clients'.

§4. Internal EPO Own Requirements

I. BEST Implementation

124. Under Articles 16 and 17 of the EPC 1973 the Receiving Section and Search Divisions were located in the branch at The Hague, and the older Protocol on Centralization referred to the taking over of the tasks of the former IIB by the branch at The Hague.

125. The initial organizational structures of the EPO[30] were based on the assumption – arising from political and historical factors, since the paper search documentation was located in the former IIB in The Hague – that searching process must be carried out by the examiners in DG 1 at The Hague, and substantive examination by the DG 2 examiners in Munich.

126. The use of newly developed electronic search tools made possible and also strongly recommendable from procedural point of view to carry out searches in Munich too and in this respect the implementation of the pilot project called BEST, with the aim of improving quality and efficiency by making it possible for the search and examination activity be performed by the same examiner, wherever he/she is located, in The Hague, Berlin or Munich, imposed the legal environment which enabled the performing of such complex task.

127. Once the request for examination is received, the same search examiner is also appointed as a member of the Examining Division who performs the required substantive examination of the European Patent under the EPC (EP) application.

128. Thus, in order to enable the office-wide implementation of the BEST procedure in Munich,[31] The Hague and Berlin, Articles 16 and 17 EPC 1973 and Section I of the Protocol on Centralization have been amended by removing the geographical allocation of the Receiving Section and Search Divisions to the branch at The Hague.

129. The allocation of the Receiving Section to the branch at The Hague in Article 16 EPC 1973 has been deleted and the allocation of the Search Divisions to the branch at The Hague in Article 17 EPC has also been deleted so that duties of that department can be run under the aegis of DG 2 in Munich and staff of the

30. Griset Pascal- The European Patent A European Success Story for Innovation; pg. 125–131; Käsel Buch 2013.
31. EPO CA/100/00 e; Basic Proposal for the Revision of The European Patent Convention.

Receiving Section who carry out the examination on filing and as to formal requirements can be assigned to either DG 1 or DG 2, depending on where the search is carried out.

130. Similarly, the Search Divisions can also be set up at the office's headquarters in Munich, allowing office-wide implementation – in Munich, The Hague and Berlin – of the BEST procedure.

131. In line with these considerations and to ensure greater flexibility in the allocation of competence within the EPO from one department to another, the limitation in time of the Receiving Section's responsibility has been also deleted.

132. The whole approach should also be considered in connection with the amended Protocol on Staff Complement (*see* Chapter 4 §7) meant to ensure that the ratio of staff at The Hague to the total EPO staff complement remains substantially unchanged after the office-wide introduction of BEST.

II. Priority Documents

133. Under the EPC 1973, if a priority document was not in an official EPO language, then a translation of the priority document had to be supplied within the same time limit as that set for paying the grant fee and filing translations of the accepted claims into the other two EPO official languages.

134. Under the EPC 2000,[32] the translation of the priority document will be normally not required. However, when relevant to assess the patentability of the claimed invention, that is, in cases where the priority date of an invention needs to be checked because of the existence of a publication between the priority date and the filing date, or the existence of another European patent application having a priority or filing date between the priority date and the filing date of the application in question could make necessary that translation. In this situation, the examiner will issue a request for a translation.

135. The relaxation of the requirement concerning translations of priority documents provides a significant administrative simplification and cost savings to applicants from countries which are not English, German or French-speaking. This is particularly so when an application claims more than one priority.

§5. Flexibility of the EPC

136. Two main approaches followed during the preparatory work and enacted by the Diplomatic Conference proved to be extremely beneficiary for implementing

32. EPO CA/100/00 e; Basic Proposal for the Revision of The European Patent Convention.

future steps in adapting the European patent system to endogen and exogen factors in a more efficient and responsive manner.

137. The first approach consisted of transferring a significant number of procedural matters from the text of the convention itself to the Implementing Regulations, thus allowing an easier and smooth future revisions, since the Implementing Regulations are under the powers of the AC.

138. Thus, it has been considered that[33] 'the EPC contains many provisions which may be subject to change for a number of reasons. Transferring these provisions to the Implementing Regulations whenever possible would allow the EPO to retain a maximum amount of flexibility by enabling the AC to respond quickly to such needs for change. For example, as the inexorable trend towards electronic filing, digital data processing and office automation continues, it is increasingly anachronistic to have references in the EPC to written documents … '.

139. Among others, here, the waiving could be exemplified to the Implementing Regulations of many conditions mentioned in previous Articles 90 to 97 and 99 to 110, 115, 117, 119 to 122 EPC such as the time limits for filing the examination request or a petition for *restitutio in integrum*.

140. The second one is provided in Articles 33 and 35 EPC 2000 which were revised just to grant competence to the AC to amend significant parts of the EPC provisions concerning patent law and procedural law (Parts II to VIII and Part X EPC – *see* next Chapter 3) in order to ensure that the EPC is in line with international treaties and community legislation on patents.

141. However, severe conditions meant to avoid possible contradictory or disputable decisions taken by the AC are provided based on conjectural majorities of interests expressed by corresponding votes. Thus, a unanimity of the Contracting States is first required to vote for the decisions which the AC is empowered to take under Article 33, paragraph 1(b). Even more, in order[34] 'to ensure the sovereignty of the Member States and the rights of the national legislative bodies in particular', the AC shall take such decisions only if all the Contracting States are represented and a decision shall not take effect if a Contracting State declares, within twelve months of date of the decision, that it does not wish to be bound by that decision.

142. The mentioned approaches should be beneficial for the end users of European patent system because they allow the EPC to be kept updated flexibly more on implementing the approaches of professionals and less under political needs for a Diplomatic Conference.

---

33. EPO CA/16/98 from 18 Feb. 1998; Points for a Revision of the European Patent Convention.
34. AIPPI- Report on the Diplomatic Conference for the Revision of the European Patent Convention. Munich, 20–29 Nov. 2000.

143. In fact,[35] 'this new power will enable the EPC to be amended where consensus has already been reached at the EU, WIPO or WTO without the need for a separate Diplomatic Conference and subsequent national ratification'.

35. N. Fox A Guide to the EPC 2000, CIPA, p. 20

Chapter 3. Basic Provisions of the Current EPC

§1. Preliminaries

144. This chapter is intended to analyse exclusively, the current text of the convention itself.[36] As previously explained, the Implementing Regulations and the basic protocols are also an integral part of the convention, but for pragmatic reasons, they will be analysed separately in Chapter 4.

145. An overall view on the EPC should, therefore, include information from all these chapters.

146. The goal of this chapter is in no way to present all the 164 articles of the EPC but to limit and focus our analysis on those which are defining the functionality of the European patent system. However, it follows the general structure of the articles of the EPC by making, whenever considered necessary, reference to the articles of the Implementing Regulation or Protocols.

§2. Legal Nature and Content

147. The EPC which established the EPOrg constitutes[37] a special agreement within the meaning of Article 19 of the convention for the Protection of Industrial Property signed in Paris on 20 March 1883 (last revised on 14 July 1967) and also a regional patent treaty within the meaning of Article 45, paragraph 1 of the PCT of 19 June 1970,

148. The EPC is indeed an 'international treaty' which should be interpreted[38] 'in harmony with the principles developed by the international public law. Under this term – treaty – it is a room for understanding not only the international agreements regulating rapports between states, but also inter-state conventions comprising and directly defining the rights and obligations for physical and moral private law persons (treaties – laws)'.

149. Consequently,[39] 'there are two characteristics which together built up the real and main originality of the EPC 1973, namely; on the one side the status of a classical international treaty – concluded between the plenipotentiaries of the European states within an intergovernmental and diplomatic conference and the ratified

36. Convention on the Grant of European Patents (European Patent Convention) of 5 Oct. 1973 as revised by the Act revising Art. 63 EPC of 17 Dec. 1991 and the Act revising the EPC of 29 Nov. 2000, 16th Edition, June 2016.
37. PREAMBLE at the European Patent Convention 1973.
38. G 006/83 OJ EPO 1985.
39. Eskil Waage- L'application de principes generaux de procedure en droit europeen des brevets, pg. 4, Litec 2000.

by national Parliaments – and– a regional law treaty, acting on a limited area, formulated in a very specific manner and instituting – according to the article 1 of the EPC – a right common to the Contracting states in the area of granting patents of invention'.

150. EPC 1973 is[40] neither a convention concluded within the framework of the European Council nor an EC Regulation or 'an action of the Community', within the understanding of Article 235 of the Rome Treaty.

151. Consequently,[41] in proceedings before the EPO, the only valid law is that which is enshrined in the EPOrg's legal system and in particular, that which set out in the convention establishing the organization or drawn up by the latter's competent organs. It includes neither the national laws of the organization's Member States nor any standards or directives drawn up by communities of States such as the European Community. At most, these may give the competent legislative body of the EPOrg grounds for reviewing the law applicable to the organization to see whether or not it should be adapted to divergent rulings in the Member States or in existing communities of States

152. This native legal system is built up[42] by the EPC at large and also by a big number of texts issued by the AC, the President and the Vice-presidents of the EPO (VP), and by the Boards of Appeal; thus, making it a complex legal order, regularly completed by texts.

§3. General and Institutional Provisions

I. General Provisions

153. The EPC establishes a system of law, for the grant of patents for invention, common to the Contracting States.[43]

154. The system of law established by the EPC is[44] an international unitary law which is valid for the activity of the EPO and of the Member States. By introducing the provisions of the EPC in a national patent law, the unitary character of the law does not lose its international oriented character.

---

40. Eskil Waage- L'application de principes generaux de procedure en droit europeen des brevets, pg. 4–5, Litec 2000.
41. D 3/98, OJ EPO 1991,257, pt. 4.
42. Eskil Waage- L'application de principes generaux de procedure en droit europeen des brevets, p. 5, Litec 2000.
43. EPC, Art. 1.
44. Stauder, Dieter, Margarete Singer – The European Patent Convention, pg. 12; Carl Heymanns Verlag KG 2003.

155. Patents granted under the provisions of the EPC are called European patents (EP).[45]

156. The grant of an EP may be requested for one or more of the Contracting States.

157. It is considered that [46] as from its grant, the EP arises as a bundle of patents, subject to the designation of more than one Member State of the EU (MS) and remains as such, contrary to the interpretation that it would rather transform itself into such a bundle.

158. The 'grandfathers' of the EPC 1973 intended to build up a community patent which automatically was requested for all community, but[47] 'as this turned out to be impossible, the scope was reduced to a system for the grant of patents for one or more states'.

159. The EP, in each of the Contracting States for which it is granted the effect of,[48] is subject to the same conditions as a national patent granted by that state unless this convention provides otherwise.

160. The granted EP is therefore not a substitute of the national patent but an alternative title of protection, at the choice of the applicant.

161. According to Article 3 EPC, the applicant [49] is required to choose the number and also, the selection of the MS and accordingly it determines the territorial effect of the EP application and its related patent.

162. The EPC also establishes[50] the EPOrg with administrative and financial autonomy having the main task of granting EPs

163. The EPOrg has two basic organs, namely: an executive body, the EPO, supervised by the AC as a legislative and managing body, whose tasks and structure are further detailed.

164. It has been expressed that[51] 'a European international organisation such as the EPO cannot be considered as a European agency because it is not set up by secondary legislation'.

45. EPC Art. 2.
46. Stauder, Dieter, Margarete Singer – The European Patent Convention, pg. 12; Carl Heymanns Verlag KG 2003.
47. Visser Derek –The Annotated European Patent Convention, pg. 10, 21 revised edition. H.TEL, Publisher 2013.
48. EPC, Art. 2(2).
49. Stauder, Dieter, Margarete Singer – The European Patent Convention, pg. 13; Carl Heymanns Verlag KG 2003.
50. EPC Art. 4.
51. EPIN- Work paper no. 19/October 2007 Governance of the EU. Debate on European Agencies.

165. By the Act revising the EPC of 29 November 2000, the new Article 4a has been inserted, providing that: ' a conference of ministers of the Contracting States responsible for patent matters shall meet at least every five years to discuss issues pertaining to the Organisation and to the European patent system'.

166. It clearly intends to provide a legal basis for regular intergovernmental conferences of the Contracting States such as those held in 1999 in London and respectively in 2000 in Munich, which led to 'the London Agreement on Translations', and the EPLA.

167. Such conferences[52] are not organs of the EPOrg themselves and neither do they affect the existing powers of the EPO and its AC. But although their decisions are not legally binding to the EPO, issued mandates may set certain objectives for the EPO. Also, these conferences could constitute a real forum of debates relating to improvements within the European patent system, outside necessary rigid mandates.

II. The EPOrg

A. *Status*

168. The organization has legal personality,[53] has its headquarters in Munich, Germany and a branch at The Hague, Netherlands[54] and is represented by the President of the EPO.[55]

169. The EPOrg is[56] 'an international, intergovernmental organization, based on the separation of powers principle, which the sovereign contracting states have entrusted with the exercise of some of their national powers in the field of patents'.

170. Subject to further more detailed presentation, it is important to clarify the equation of power and the distribution of responsibilities in the EPOrg between the EPO, its President and the AC.

171. In this respect, it has been interpreted that [57] 'the EPC assigns executive power to the EPO to grant patents and to its President to manage the EPO in organizational respects, while to the Administrative Council it assigns limited legislative powers restricted to lower-ranking rules along with financial and supervisory powers'.

---

52. N. Fox A Guide to the EPC 2000, CIPA 2007, pg. 2.
53. EPC, Art. 5.
54. EPC Art. 6(1).
55. EPC Art. 5(3).
56. G 3/08 OJ 2011.
57. EPO Case Law of the Boards of Appeal VII 1.1; 8th Edition July 2016.

B. Membership

172. Currently there are thirty-eight Contracting States of the EPC and accordingly, the EPOrg has thirty-eight members and the following list indicates the date of the entry into force of the EPC for the relevant states: AL (1 May 2010), AT(1 May 1979), BE (7 October 1977), BG (1 July 2002), CH (7 October 1977), CY (1 April 1998), CZ (1 July 2002), DE (7 October 1977), DK (1 January 1990), EE(1 July 2002), ES (1 October 1986), FI (1 March 1996), FR (7 October 1977), GB (7 October 1977), GR (1 October 1986), HR (1 January 2008), HU (1 January 2003), IE (1 August 1992), IS (1 November 2004), IT (1 December 1978), LI (1 April 1980), LT(1 December 2004), LU (7 October 1977), LV (1 July 2005), MC (1 December 1991), MK (1 January 2009), MT (1 March 2007), NL (7 October 1977), NO (1 January 2008), PL (1 March 2004), PT (1 January 1992), RO (1 March 2003), RS (1 October 2010), SE (1 May 1978), SI (1 December 2002), SK (1 July 2002), SM (1 July 2009), TR (1 November 2000).

173. As can be easily seen, twenty-six of the mentioned states are MS, the other remaining twelve illustrating de facto that the EPO and EPOrg are not EU institutions and neither assimilated

174. Nevertheless, European patent protection may also be requested for the so-called extension states, which although are not Contracting States to the EPC, have instead signed and enforced 'extension agreements', under which the protection conferred by European patent applications and patents may be extended to the mentioned countries, namely Bosnia-Herzegovina since 1 December 2004 and Montenegro, since 1 March 2010.

175. An extension agreement is an international treaty between the EPOrg and an extension state which the President of the EPO is authorized by the AC to conclude with the council's approval,[58] providing to applicants a simple route to patent protection in the extension states and enabling the extension state to the possibility of a patent protection for its territory by extending the effects of European as well as Procedures under the PCT before the EPO (EURO-PCT) applications and patents.

176. As a matter of fact, the extension system began effectively in 1993 with Slovenia and later on, some other countries: Romania, Lithuania, Latvia, Croatia, Macedonia, Albania and Serbia chose to have the status of 'extension state', prior to and as a preliminary step for joining the EPC.

177. Since 2010, it has concluded further agreements providing for European patents to have effect in Non-contracting States. It is to be mentioned that these 'validation agreements' are not limited to European countries like the Republic of

58. EPC Art. 33(4).

Moldova (1 November 2015), but currently, an agreement has been signed and entered into force with Morocco (1 March 2015) but has not yet been ratified with Tunisia and Cambodia.

178. If the applicant requests extension/validation and pays the extension/validation fee(s) in time, it can have European patent applications and patents extended to/validated in these countries, where they will then, in principle, have the same effect as national applications and patents and will be subject to national law and will enjoy essentially the same protection as patents the EPO grants for the EPC Contracting States.

179. In conclusion, one can currently request an extension to Bosnia-Herzegovina and to Montenegro and validation in Morocco and in the Republic of Moldova.

180. In principle, the extension and validation systems are largely the same as the designation system for Contracting States. It is, however, to be noted that the extension and validation systems are based not on direct application of the EPC but solely on the relevant national law modelled on the EPC. Hence, they are subject to the national extension/validation rules of the country concerned

C. Institutional Matters

181. In each of the Contracting States, the organization shall enjoy the most extensive legal capacity accorded to legal persons under the national law of that state; it may, in particular, acquire or dispose of movable and immovable property and may be a party to legal proceedings.

182. The conditions under which the members of the AC, the employees of the EPO, and such other specified persons to take part in the work of the EPOrg shall enjoy, in each Contracting State, the privileges and immunities[59] necessary for the performance of their duties, are defined in the Protocol on Privileges and Immunities annexed to the EPC (*see* Chapter 4 §4).

183. In a dedicated Article 9, EPC provides specific conditions ensuring current liability and respectively non-current, including personal liability of the staffs of the EPO.

184. Thus, the contractual liability[60] of the organization is governed by the law applicable to the contract in question, jurisdiction to settle any dispute being courts of the Federal Republic of Germany, except for the parties designated under the current terms which will be settled by the court of another state.

59. EPC Art. 8.
60. EPC Art. 9.

185. The non-contractual liability of the organization in respect of any damage caused by it or by its employees in the performance of their duties will be governed by the law of the Federal Republic of Germany, or depending on where the damage is caused, by the branch at The Hague or a sub-office or employees attached thereto, by the law of the Contracting State in which such branch or sub-office is located. Consequently, any dispute will be settled, as the case may be, by the courts of the Federal Republic of Germany or of the state in which the branch or sub-office is located

186. The Service Regulations or conditions of employment, according to internal issued documents, governs the personal liability of the employees of the EPO towards the organization.

III. The EPO

A. *Premises and Staff*

187. In compliance with the provisions of the EPC,[61] the EPO is located in Munich, Germany with a branch at The Hague, Netherlands, currently located in Rijswijk.

188. The possibility provided for in the EPC,[62] to create, by decisions of the AC and subject to the approval of the Contracting State or organization concerned, sub-offices of the EPO, for the purpose of information and liaison in the Contracting States and with intergovernmental organizations in the field of industrial property, has been gradually materialized by the setting up of procedural sub-offices in Berlin, Germany in 1978 and respectively in Vienna, Austria, and a 'liaison bureau' in Brussels, Belgium, enabling direct connection with EU and support for innovation and competiveness.

189. The sub-office in Berlin was created under Protocol on Centralization (*see* Chapter 4 §5) which is also a filing office, and the one in Vienna, which is not a filing office, is oriented towards patent information access and policy.

190. The EPC regulates staffing arrangements and the legal status of the EPO employees by relating itself to various aspects of employment and activity. They refer to:

- their privileges and immunities (*see* Chapter 4 §4);
- the supervisory authority of the President[63] and appointment of superior staff;[64]

61. EPC, Art. 6(2).
62. EPC, Art. 7.
63. EPC Art. 10(2)f.
64. EPC, Art. 11.

– employees' duties of confidentiality;[65]
– disputes.[66]

1. Further Details

191. Noticeably, the EPO is the second-largest intergovernmental organization in Europe, employing [67] approximately 6,800 staff from over 30 countries, of which, approximately 4,300 are patent examiners and approximately 140 are members of the Boards of Appeal.

192. However, the EPO is not a legal entity as such, acting only as mentioned, as the executive body of the EPOrg, which does have a legal personality.

B. Responsibility and Task

193. This subject matter will be discussed further in detail, but it is conclusively obvious that in its capacity as executive body, the EPO is mainly responsible for searching, examining and publishing patent applications, for holding opposition proceedings, and respectively for appeal proceedings before the Boards of Appeal.

194. Besides the specific procedures for granting European patents, the EPO is also in charge of establishing search reports for national patent applications on behalf of the Patent Offices of France, Netherlands, Belgium, Luxembourg, Italy, Turkey, Greece, Cyprus, Malta, San Marino, Lithuania, Latvia, and Monaco. These new tasks were implemented based on bilateral agreements signed by the EPO with national authorities of these Member States and are performed on commercial bases.

195. Another important task of the EPO, provided for in the EPC,[68] is that at the request of the competent national court hearing an infringement or revocation action, the EPO must give a technical opinion concerning the European patent which is the subject of the action.

C. Management and Structure

196. The EPO is managed by the President,[69] who is responsible for its activities to the AC. According to what has been already mentioned, the President also represents the EPOrg and therefore, he/she has a dual role: representative of the EPOrg and head of the EPO.

65. EPC, Art. 12.
66. EPC, Art. 14.
67. EPO- Social Report for the year 2016; pg. 8–9.
68. EPO Art.25.
69. EPO Art. 10.

197. EPC provides[70] for the President a series of functions and powers enabling him to fulfil important managerial duties, but on external activity [71] 'It is not clear to what extent the President can direct EPO in any external activity not directly related to one of the powers of functions listed in Art. 10(2) without the supervision of the Administrative Council.'

198. In particular, he/she must take necessary measures to ensure the proper functioning of the EPO; to split duties to be performed at the EPO in Munich and its branch, including sub-offices respectively; to submit to the AC, proposals for amending the EPC, general regulations, or decisions which come within the competence of the AC; and to appoint and/or promote the employees, including the exercise of the supervisory and disciplinary authority over the employees, others than senior employees which are specifically appointed by the AC. Within his/her natural interlinked relation with the AC, the President of the EPO prepares, presents for approval, and implements the budget of the EPO and submits a yearly management report to it.

199. The EPC does not provide the numbers of VPs but gives the possibility to any of them to temporarily take the place of the President if he is absent or indisposed, or if he delegated his functions and powers, in accordance with the procedure laid down by the AC.

200. The EPC stipulates a specific mechanism for the appointment of senior employees[72] where the AC has a decisive role. Thus, the President of the EPO itself is appointed by the AC.

201. The AC also (re)appoints VPs, the members, including the Chairpersons of the Boards of Appeal and of the Enlarged Board of Appeal at the proposal of the President of the EPO or, for re-elections, after he has been consulted. The AC, after consulting the President of the EPO, may also appoint, as members of the Enlarged Board of Appeal, legally qualified members of the national courts or quasi-judicial authorities of the Contracting States, who may continue their judicial activities at the national level.

202. Accordingly, the AC is in charge of exercising disciplinary authority over the President of the EPO and other high-ranking employees which it (re)appointed.

203. Legal bases for structural organization and functioning are also to be found in the EPC,[73] which provides that the structure of the EPO entrusted to carry out the specific procedures will comprise of:

---

70. EPC Art. 10.
71. Visser Derek –The Annotated European Patent Convention, pg. 16; 21 revised edition. H.TEL, Publisher 2013.
72. EPC Art. 11.
73. EPC Art. 15.

(a) A Receiving Section, responsible[74] for the examination on filing and formal requirements of European patent applications.
(b) Search Divisions, responsible[75] for drawing up European search reports.
(c) Examining Divisions, responsible[76] for the examination of European patent applications and also for issuing technical opinion concerning the European patent which is the subject of an action at national level, as previously mentioned. As a rule, each division consists of three technically qualified examiners, but if the nature of the decision requires such a measure, it may be enlarged with a fourth examiner who is legally qualified. However, before a decision is taken on a European patent application, its examination shall, as a general rule, be entrusted to one member of the Examining Division.
(d) Opposition Divisions, responsible[77] for the examination of oppositions against any European patent; as a rule, it consists of three technically qualified examiners, subject to condition that at least two of them have not taken part in the proceedings for grant of the patent to which the opposition relates and that an examiner who has taken part in the proceedings for the grant of the European patent may not be the Chairman. If it is considered that the nature of the decision requires such a measure, it may be supplemented by a legally qualified examiner who shall not have taken part in the proceedings for grant of the patent.
(e) A Legal Division responsible[78] for decisions in respect of entries in the Register of European Patents and in respect of registration on, and deletion from, the list of professional representatives; decisions are taken by one legally qualified member;
(f) Boards of Appeal, responsible[79] for the examination of appeals from decisions of:
    (f1) the Receiving Section, each Board of Appeal consisting of three legally qualified members;
    (f2) the Examining Divisions, any Board of Appeal consisting, as the case might be, of: two technically qualified members and one legally qualified member, when the decision concerns the refusal of a European patent application or the grant, limitation or revocation of a European patent, and was taken by an Examining Division consisting of less than four members, or three technically and two legally qualified members, when the decision was taken by an Examining Division consisting of four members, or when the Board of Appeal considers that the nature of the appeal so requires, and three legally qualified members in all other cases;
    (f3) the Opposition Divisions, any Board of Appeal consisting of two technically qualified members and one legally qualified member, when the decision was taken by an Opposition Division consisting of three members, or three technically and two legally qualified members, when the decision

74. EPC Art. 16.
75. EPC Art. 17.
76. EPC Art. 18.
77. EPC Art. 19.
78. EPC Art. 20.
79. EPC Art. 21.

was taken by an Opposition Division of four members, or when the Board of Appeal considers that the nature of the appeal so requires;

(f4) the Legal Division, each Board of Appeal consisting of three legally qualified members.

(g) An Enlarged Board of Appeal, responsible[80] for:

(g1) deciding on points of law referred to it by Boards of Appeal;

(g2) giving opinions on points of law referred to it by the President of the EPO;

(g3) deciding on petitions for review of decisions of the Boards of Appeal.

In proceedings under paragraph g1 and g2, the structure of the Enlarged Board of Appeal consists of five legally and two technically qualified members and in proceedings under paragraph g3, of three or five members as laid down in the Implementing Regulations, a legally qualified member being the Chairman in all situations.

204. The members of the Enlarged Board of Appeal and of the Boards of Appeal are appointed[81] for a term of five years, their duty being, only for exceptional cases, shorter due to a decision taken by the AC on a proposal from the Enlarged Board of Appeal, or by their resignation or retirement.

205. The members of the boards may not be members of other division of the EPO, and in their decisions, they shall comply only with the provisions of the EPC. They are not bounded by any other instructions of regulations.

206. The EPO case law held that[82] 'these EPC provisions which are governing the independence of members of the boards of appeal, their competence and method of work, and the nature of the decisions they take, indicate that the boards act as courts with the task of ensuring that the law is respected when the EPC is applied. Moreover, there is no appeal against decisions of the boards'.

207. According to a recent decision of the AC,[83] a new structure of the office has been approved which rely on three main Directorates-General, headed by VPs: DG 1 'Patent Granting Process', DG 2 'Corporate Services', and DG 3 'Legal and International Affairs'.

208. DG 1 brought the Search, Examination, and Opposition Divisions and the Receiving Section into a single Directorate-General, whereby VP1 was established.

209. Its operational functions are based on the regrouping of the cluster structure into three enlarged Principal Directorates (PDs), according to technology

80. EPC Art. 22.
81. EPC Art. 23.
82. EPO Case Law of the Boards of Appeal VII 1.2.1; 8th Edition July 2016.
83. EPO CA/65/17; Munich, 09.06.2017.

('Mobility and Mechatronics', 'Healthcare, Biotechnology and Chemistry', 'Information and Communications Technology'), each one headed by a Chief Operating Officer (COO).

210. Moreover, each PD will comprise of twenty-five Directorates of more than sixty examiners and typically between five and nine Formalities Officers, depending on tasks, fields and size of the directorate. Each directorate would be headed by a Director reporting to the COO. Each PD will further contain one or two dedicated Opposition and Central Formalities Directorates.

211. Several services in DG 1 and DG 2 currently providing the support to the operations, the customer relations and also, the quality management system merged into three PDs: PD User Support and Quality Management, PD Business Services, and PD Automation Support, all directly linked to VP1.

212. The operations in the new DG 1 will rely on new big entities: three main PDs, each counting up to around 1,500 staff member in total, covering several enlarged directorates (sixty to eighty staff members per new directorate, compared to thirty in the current structure).

213. DG 2 'Corporate Services' concentrates all the non-operational support functions, which are often in regular exchanges, fostering their coordination.

214. DG 3 'Legal and International Affairs' is composed of the former DG 5, with the specific addition of operational responsibility for the Unitary Patent and a directorate to centralize logistical support for external events.

D. Languages of the EPO

215. Article 14 EPC on languages of the EPO stipulates that there are three official languages: English, French and German. This means that a European patent application must be filed in one of these languages, which will be used, in principle, in all proceedings before the office, for the publication of European patent applications and of the specifications of European patents. However, these specifications have to include a translation of the claims in the other two official languages of the EPO. These three official languages are, therefore 'procedural languages'.

216. The EPC however offers a certain flexibility in the language restriction framework by giving the possibility to fill the patent application in any language, subject to later filing of a translation, and considering a certain privilege regime for the so-called admissible non-EPO languages, namely the official languages of the EPC Contracting States, other than the three official ones.

217. Accordingly, on the terminology of the languages,[84] the EPC makes a distinction between three groups of languages:

- official; languages of the EPO (English, French. German);
- procedural languages that are used in the proceedings before the EPO;
- official languages of the MS, that are not one of the official languages.

218. Natural or legal persons having their residence or principal place of business within a Contracting State having a language other than English, French, or German as an official language and nationals of that state who are resident abroad may file documents which have to be filed within a time limit in an official language of that state. They shall, however, file a translation in an official language of the EPO in prescribed conditions. If any document, other than those documents making up the European patent application, is not filed in the prescribed language or if any required translation is not filed in due time, the document shall be deemed not to have been filed.

219. Throughout the proceedings before the EPO, such translation may be brought into conformity with the application as filed. If a required translation is not filed in due time, the application shall be deemed to be withdrawn.

220. Based on these presumptions, we may conclude that there are three situations in which a translation of the European application will be required:

- the European application was filed in a language which is not an official language of the EPO;
- the European application was filed by reference to a previously filed application which is not in an official language of the EPO;[85]
- the European divisional application was filed in the same language as the earlier (parent) application on which it is based, where this was not an official language of the EPO.[86]

221. Official publications of the EPO are published in the three official languages of the EPO namely the European Patent Bulletin, the Official Journal of the EPO. Also, entries in the European Patent Register are made in the three official languages of the EPO, the entry in the language of the proceedings being considered as authentic in cases of doubt.

84. Stauder, Dieter, Margarete Singer – The European Patent Convention, pg. 39; Carl Heymanns Verlag KG 2003.
85. EPC Rule 40(3).
86. EPC Rule 36(2).

IV. The AC

A. Composition and Committees

222. It is the legislative body of the EPOrg and in this capacity, it supervises the activities of the office, appoints the President of the EPO and votes on the office's budget

223. The AC is composed[87] of one representative and one alternate representative of each Contracting States and may be assisted by advisers or experts.

224. The vast majority of the representatives are top managers of the National Patent Offices (NPOs) of the MS, but there are (few) situations where according to their national legislation, representatives are appointed at the level of managers in the coordinating ministry of the Patent Office.

225. EPC also provides that the meetings of the AC may also be attended by observers,[88] currently by:[89]

- observer states, which currently Bosnia and Herzegovina (BA) are and Montenegro (ME);
- intergovernmental organizations: EU, WIPO, European Union Intellectual Property Office (EUIPO), and Nordic Patent Institute (NPI);
  and
- some non-governmental organizations: Institute of Professional Representatives before the EPO (EPI), and BusinessEurope.

226. EPC leaves a certain freedom for the AC to decide invitation of other possible observers.

227. Chairmanship[90] of the AC is ensured by a Chairperson and a Deputy Chairman from among the representatives and alternate representatives of the Contracting States, elected for a term of three years, with possibility for re-election.

1. Board B28

228. Based on Article 28 which allows the setting up of a specific board of the AC, 'Board B28' has been established, which must perform the duties assigned by the AC in accordance with the Rules of Procedure; to be further detailed.

---

87. EPC Art. 26.
88. EPC Art. 30.
89. EPO-Administrative Council-Composition; https://www.epo.org/about-us/governance/administrative-council/composition.html.
90. EPC Art. 27.

229. The Board B28, as the Board of Administrative Council[91] has a current mandate to[92] assist the Chairman of the AC in preparing and ensuring the continuity of the work of the council, particularly in:

- preparing the council's work programme;
- general coordination of the work of the council and its bodies, on the basis of the work programme;
- facilitating cohesion and consensus within the EPOrg.

230. The Chairman regularly drafts reports to the council on the board's activities.

231. Participants in the Board B28 are:

- Chairman and Deputy Chairman of the AC, as members ex officio.
- Honorary Chairman of the AC.
- Three members of the AC, elected by the AC, for a term of three years, without the possibility of re-election.
- Chairman of the Budget and Finance Committee (BFC).
- Chairman of the Technical and Operational Support Committee (TOSC).
- Chairman of the Committee on Patent Law.
- Chairman of the Select Committee.
- President of the EPO.

232. In its composition, a list of representatives of other committees appear and in order to present their goal, it should be mentioned that in its extremely complex activity, the AC is assisted and advised from legal, financial, technical, and administrative points of view by these specific committees.

2. Budget and Finance Committee

233. The BFC is set up under Article 3 of the Financial Regulations of the EPOrg and advise the AC on:

- proposals relating to the amendment of fees laid down in the EPC or its Implementing Regulations;
- on financial matters concerning revision of the EPC and its constituents;
- on financial policy of the EPOrg including its bodies and the EPO;
- on financial matters which may affect the EPC or on financial aspects implied by the cooperation with and among the Contracting States;
- on any financial question relating to the European patent system, including Unitary Patent system, requested by either the AC or the President of the EPO.

---

91. EPO CA/D 4/03 and CA/D 10/03.
92. EPO-B28 Board of the Administrative Council; ttps://www.epo.org/about-us/governance/administrative-council/bodies/b28.html.

3. Committee on Patent Law

234. The Committee on Patent Law advise the AC:[93]

- on proposals relating to the amendment of time limits laid down in the EPC or the amendment of its Implementing Regulations;
- on legal matters concerning revision of the EPC;
- on harmonization of national law in the Contracting States relating to the implementation of the EPC;
- on matters on international patent law which may affect the EPC or on cooperation of the Contracting States, pursuant to the preamble of the EPC;
- on any legal question relating to the European patent system, requested by either the AC or the President of the EPO.

4. Technical and Operational Support Committee

235. The TOSC provides the AC with[94] opinions on operational aspects of the following matters:

- technical information and infrastructure, especially information dissemination in particular provides proposals for guidelines on the production of and access to patent information data for use by offices or the public and evaluation of infrastructure elements supporting the exchange and dissemination of technical information
- trilateral technical cooperation EPO-USPTO-JPO, as well as other forms of technical cooperation in international fora, in particular,monitoring and examining technical cooperation projects in the perspective of the European patent system and the preservation of its interests and making suitable contributions to support the EPO in preparing the technical and operational aspects of the decisions to be taken by the council;
- operational issues concerning quality, especially monitoring of the European Quality System and other technical arrangements on patent procedure results;
- informing and supporting the council on technical issues regarding the European Patent Network, within the policy framework defined by the council;
- providing advice to the council on any further technical matters.

5. Supervisory Board of the Academy

236. The Supervisory Board of the Academy[95] is a managing body of the European Patent Academy and is in charge of:

93. EPO Council Bodies; www.epo.org/about-us/governance/administrative-council/bodies/patent-law.
94. EPO Council Bodies; www.epo.org/about-us/governance/administrative-council/bodies/support-committee.html.
95. European Patent Academy set up according to CA/D 10/04 and CA/D 4/14.

- adopting the strategic guidelines for the Academy based on proposals made by the President of the Office;
- giving an opinion on the draft for the annual work programme of the Academy and on the draft for annual budget proposal of the Academy;
- approving when necessary and after consulting the President of the Office, setting up of ad hoc working parties, organizations contributing to the financing of a project, the EPI and educational institutions;
- adopting a policy regarding tuition fees;
- giving an opinion on and endorse the reports on the activities of the Academy;
- appointing experts in IP education and training;
- presenting regularly the results of the monitoring and evaluation procedure regarding the activity of the Academy to the AC.

6. Select Committee

237. The Select Committee[96] is in charge of supervising the EPO's activities related to the tasks entrusted to it in the context of unitary patent protection (UPP) and in particular, of the setting of fees due to the procedures specific to the Unitary Patent system.

238. The last committee is the Boards of Appeal Committee,[97] which advises and assists the AC in its supervisory duties relating to the Boards of Appeal Unit.

B. Competence and Procedural Aspects

239. EPC provides[98] that it is mandatory for the AC 'to hold an ordinary meeting once each year' and 'to meet on the initiative of its Chairman or at the request of one-third of the Contracting States'. Practice of the past years shows certain regularity in holding these meetings (namely four meetings/year or one/ trimester), of which, the meetings in June and December are usually richer in decisions than those in March and September. Meetings of the AC are convened by its Chairman and whenever the case and the legal conditions are fulfilled, additional meetings may be convened.

240. The President of the EPO takes part in the deliberations of the AC which are based on agreed agenda, and are held in accordance with its Rules of Procedure.

241. The agenda contains questions requested by any Contracting State in accordance with the Rules of Procedure

96. Set up by the 25 Member States participating in the unitary patent, according to Art. 9(2) of Regulation (EU) No 1257/2012 ('the Regulation') and Art. 145 EPC.
97. Set up according to CA/D 6/16 and CA/D 7/16.
98. EPC Art. 29.

242. The official languages of the EPO, English, French and German are equally[99] used in the deliberations of the AC as well as those of the documents submitted to the AC and the minutes of its deliberations.

243. EPC provides[100] a major competence to the AC which must be coherent with that of the President in what usually is called as 'a duality of powers'; it covers:

(a) amending significant parts if the EPC namely:
  – the time limits laid down in the convention;
  – Parts II to VIII and Part X of the convention, in order to bring them into line with EU legislation and international treaty relating to patents;
  – the Implementing Regulations.

(b) adopting and amending, in conformity with the convention:
  – the Financial Regulations;
  – the Service Regulations for permanent employees and the conditions of employment of other employees of the EPO, their salary scales, granting supplementary benefits;
  – the Pension Scheme Regulations and any appropriate adjustment of the pensions to the salaries;
  – the Rules relating to Fees;
  – its Rules of Procedure.

(c) authorizing the President of the EPO to negotiate and to conclude agreements on behalf of the EPOrg with states, with intergovernmental organizations and with European documentation centers set up accordingly.

244. As presented in Chapter 3, the provision of Article 33 lit. b) enabling the AC to amend 'the Parts II to VIII and Part X of the convention' has been agreed by the Diplomatic Conference in 2000 and it is considered that,[101] 'this new power will enable the EPC to be amended where consensus has already been reached at EU, WIPO or WTO without the needs for a separate Diplomatic Conference and subsequent national ratification'.

245. It is understood[102] that the AC can exercise this competence in the case of any treaty, convention or community text containing provisions relating to patent law (e.g., the provisions of Part II, section 5 of Annex 1C (the TRIPS Agreement) to the Agreement Establishing the WTO of 15 April 1994).

246. Thus, possible delays in adopting legal and procedural matters of the EPC comparing to relevant international developments should be therefore minimized, by avoiding holding revision conferences for the sole purpose of adapting the EPC

99. EPC Art 31.
100. EPC Art. 33.
101. N. Fox A Guide to the EPC 2000, CIPA 2007, pg. 20.
102. EPO CA/PL 25/00 Rev. 1; Basic Proposal for the Revision of the European Patent Convention; Munich, 28.07.2000.

to texts already adopted by all or a majority of Contracting States. Also, national ratification procedures, always of uncertain duration and outcome, are no longer deemed indispensable for the amended wording of an EPC article to enter into force.

247. Within the framework of the same Article 34 (4) EPC, the President of the EPO concluded and signed the 'extension agreements' with the so-called extended states (*see* Chapter 3 §3 II) namely, an international treaty between the EPOrg and the extension state which the President of the EPO is authorized by the AC to conclude with the council's approval. Such an agreement provides a simple route to patent protection in the extension states by enabling it to offer patent protection for its territory by extending the effects of European and EURO-PCT applications and corresponding granted patents.

248. The extension system[103] is fully compatible with the EPC valid for Contracting States except that it is not based on direct application of the EPC but on national law modelled on the EPC and consequently the national law of the extension state governs the proceedings and the legal effects of the extension.

249. However, it should be understood that relating to their last competence, the AC may not take a decision concerning an international treaty, before its entry into force, and concerning the EU legislation, before its entry into force or before the expiry of the implementation period, as the case may be.

250. The right to vote[104] in the AC belongs exclusively to the Contracting States, which, in principle, are disposed of a single vote each. One single but relevant exception refers to the weighting of votes[105] applicable in case of the adoption or amendment of the Rules relating to Fees and the adoption of the budget or changing the budget of the organization if the financial contribution to be made by the Contracting States would be increased.

251. Based on a clear differentiation of the importance and effect taken within the AC, its decision,[106] are taken:

- by a simple majority of the Contracting States represented and voting, for usual working decisions;
- by the majority of three-quarters of the votes of the Contracting States represented and voting, required for the decisions which the AC is empowered to take on substantive financial and international matters;[107]

103. T 0007/07.
104. EPC Art. 34.
105. EPC Art. 36.
106. EPC Art. 35.
107. EPC Art. 7, Art. 11, para. 1, Art. 33, para. 1(a) and (c), and 2 to 4, Art. 39, para. 1, Art. 40, para. 2 and 4, Art. 46, Art. 134a, Art. 149a, para. 2, Art. 152, Art. 153, para. 7, Art. 166 and Art. 172.

- by unanimity of the Contracting States, voting shall be required for the decisions which the AC is empowered to take on Parts II to VIII and Part X of the convention. In this situation, the AC may take such decisions only if all the Contracting States are represented and subject to the condition that such a decision shall not take effect if a Contracting State declares, within twelve months of the date of the decision, that it does not wish to be bound by that decision.

252. The period of twelve months allows representatives of the Contracting States on the AC to confer with the national legislative bodies to ensure that the change is acceptable

V. Financial Provisions

253. The EPOrg is a self-financed organization which bases its incomes on:[108]

(a) Organization's own resources namely: all income from fees and other sources and also the reserves of the EPOrg as well as the resources of the Pension Reserve Fund. EPC provides[109] that the EPO may levy fees for any official task or procedure carried out under this convention. Time limits for the payment of fees other than those fixed by EPC and the legal consequences of failure to pay such fee in due time shall be laid down in the Implementing Regulations. The Rules relating to fees are the basis for establishing the amounts of the fees and the ways in which they are to be paid.
(b) Payments made by the Contracting States as renewal fees for European patents levied in these states; the proportion of renewal fees for European patents to be remitted to the EPOrg by the Contracting States is the same for all Contracting States and currently 50% with effect from 1 January 1985.[110] It is to be noted that the EPC provides that this proportion might be increased up to 75%, subject to the condition that the amounts of the fees and the proportion shall be fixed at such a level as to ensure that the revenue in respect thereof is sufficient for the budget of the organization to be balanced.
(c) Where necessary, by special financial contributions made by the Contracting States.

254. According to the revised Article 42(1) EPC 2000, the budget must be balanced and based on generally accepted accounting principles (GAAP) as defined in the Financial Regulations of the Organization.

108. EPC Art. 37–40.
109. EPC Art. 41.
110. Decision of the Administrative Council of 8 Jun. 1984 on the proportion of renewal fees for European patents to be remitted to the European Patent Organisation; OJ EPO 1984, pg. 296.

255. The EPOrg may consider, where appropriate, other (on small scale) incomes from supplementary tasks, borrowings on land or buildings or from third-party funding for specific projects. The special financial contributions shall be repaid with interest at a rate which shall be the same for all Contracting States.

256. The President of the EPO submits the draft budget to the AC no later than the date prescribed in the Financial Regulations and it is adopted by the AC usually at its meeting in December.

257. Budget implementation[111] is ensured by the President of the EPO in his own responsibility and within the limits of the allocated appropriations, who may, in accordance with the Financial Regulations, transfer funds between the various headings or sub-headings.

258. The income and expenditure account and a balance sheet of the organization shall be examined by independent auditors[112] appointed by the AC for a period of five years, renewable or extensible.

259. The President of the EPO submits the accounts of the preceding accounting period in respect of the budget and the balance sheet annually to the AC together with the report of the auditors. Once the AC approves the annual accounts together with the report of the auditors, the President of the EPO will be discharged in respect of the implementation of the budget.

§4. Substantive Patent Law

I. Patentable Inventions; Inventions Excluded or Excepted from Patentability

A. *Patentable Inventions*

1. General provisions

260. The EPC, in its revision of 2000 (*see* Chapter 2), was brought in full line with TRIPS on patentability matters; it provides[113] that 'European patents shall be granted for any inventions, in all fields of technology, provided that they are new, involve an inventive step and are susceptible of industrial application.'

261. There are some basic concepts on patentability expressed here, which indeed are defining the substantive patent law as regulated and implemented in Europe.

---

111. EPC Art. 48.
112. EPC Art. 49.
113. EPC Art. 52(1).

262. This means that in order to be patentable, an(y) invention must meet the following cumulative conditions:

– invention (technical), belonging to a field of technology;
– novelty;
– inventive step;
– susceptible to industrial application.

263. According to the case law, the term 'invention' is to be construed as 'subject matter having technical character',[114] a direct consequence is that the analysis if a claimed subject matter is an invention within the meaning of patentability, is in principle a prerequisite for the examination with respect to the three patentability conditions: novelty, inventive step, and industrial application since these latter requirements are defined only for inventions.[115]

264. Based on a series of individual decisions of the EPO Boards of Appeal, it concluded that the technical character of an invention is given[116] if that invention:

– relate to a technical field;
– concern a technical problem;
– has technical features in terms of which the matter for which protection is sought can be defined in the claim;
– result in a technical effect.

265. According to the EPO patenting practice, the examination of the existence of an invention[117] must be completely separated from and not confused with the examination of the other three patentability requirements. It starts from the assumption that the concept of 'invention' is a general and absolute requirement of patentability, contrary to the other three: novelty, inventive step, and industrial applicability which are considered as relative. The decisive factor for the existence of a potentially patentable invention is the inherent character of the claimed subject matter.

2. Patentable Biotechnological Inventions

266. Biotechnological inventions are inventions related to a product consisting of or containing biological material or a process by means of which biological material is produced, processed or used. They should, in principle, respect the general patentability conditions and concepts already expressed. However, in line with EU

114. T 931/95, OJ 2001.
115. T 258/03, OJ 2004.
116. Strenc Alexandru –European Software Directives and European Software Patents; pg. 123 Wolters Kluwer 2017.
117. T 154/04, OJ 2008.

legislation,[118] EPC provides special types of technical solutions on biotechnological inventions which should be patentable, if they indeed respect the said conditions and if they concern:[119]

(a) biological material which is isolated from its natural environment or produced by means of a technical process even if it previously occurred in nature;
(b) plants or animals if the technical feasibility of the invention is not confined to a particular plant or animal variety;
(c) a microbiological or other technical process, or a product obtained by means of such a process other than a plant or animal variety.

B. *Inventions Excluded from Patentability*

267. As is the case of most of the patent laws, EPC also provides the so-called negative definition of an (patentable) invention, by giving a non-exhaustive list of the subject matters of activities which:[120]

> shall not be regarded as inventions (within the meaning of patentable inventions), namely:
>
> – discoveries, scientific theories and mathematical methods;
> – aesthetic creations;
> – schemes, rules and methods for performing mental acts, playing games or doing business, and programs for computers;
> – presentations of information.

268. Exclusions of the patentability of the subject matter or activities referred to therein are nevertheless valid:[121]

> only to the extent to which a European patent application or European patent relates to such subject matter or activities as such
>
> and based on this provision has been considered that 'it was the clear intention of the contracting states that this list of "excluded" subject matter should not be given too broad a scope of application'.[122]

269. The patenting practice and jurisprudence of the EPO makes a clear and unambiguous connection between the phrase 'to belong to a field of technology' and

118. Directive 98/44/EC of the European Parliament and of the Council of 6 Jul. 1998 on the legal protection of biotechnological inventions; Official Journal of the European Communities L 213 Volume 41; 30 Jul. 1998.
119. EPC Rule 27.
120. EPC Art. 52(2).
121. EPC Art. 52(3).
122. EPO Case Law of the Boards of Appeal; I A 2.1; 8th Edition July 2016.

to 'relate to subject matters or activities as such', when stated in fact the technicality of an invention as a (pre) condition for granting a patent of that invention. More specifically, in principle, an invention which belongs to a field of technology shall not relate to a subject matter of activity as such and consequently will possess a technical character.

270. The term *as such* has no legal definition but some relevant examples given under the following subsection 1 could clarify its meaning and relation with a technical invention.

271. Of a significant importance is the conclusion that[123] 'the structure of the EPC therefore suggests that it should be possible to determine whether subject-matter was excluded under Art. 52(2) EPC without any knowledge of the state of the art, including common general knowledge'.

1. Discoveries, Scientific Theories and Mathematical Methods

272. The pure discovery of the 'COANDA effect' of attaching the fluid to solid walls or the scientific theory of restrained relativity does not have a technical character that can consequently be viewed as patentable *as such,* but the application of the effect to fluid amplifiers and logic fluid elements, or technical means to put into evidence and measure the effects of the restrained relativity became technical inventions, and thus patentable.

273. If a new property of a known material or article is found or to find a previously unrecognized substance occurring in nature are mere discoveries and non-patentable because discoveries as such have no technical effect and is therefore not an invention within the meaning of Article 52(1) EPC. If, however, that property is put to practical use or the substance found in nature can be shown to produce a technical effect, then these constitute inventions potentially patentable.

274. Following the same idea, under EPC, purely mathematical abstract or intellectual methods are not patentable but indeed, mathematical algorithm implemented in methods for controlling processes and technologies are patentable.

2. Aesthetic Creations

275. Aesthetic creations relate, by definition, to objects having features relying on aspects which are not technical and based on an essentially subjective appreciation. The aesthetic creation based on that effect itself is not patentable, neither in a product nor a process claim. Nevertheless,[124] if an aesthetic effect is obtained by a

123. EPO Case Law of the Boards of Appeal; I A 1.4; 8th Edition July 2016.
124. EPO Guidelines for examination, G–II, 3.4; November 2015.

technical structure or other technical means, although the aesthetic effect itself is not patentable, the means of obtaining it is potentially patentable.

3. Schemes, Rules and Methods for Performing Mental Acts, Playing Games or Doing Business, Program of Computers

276. Probably, the most relevant cases are within the field of software and business methods, where, from a European point of view, pure software methods and business methods are to be considered *as such and* thus, excluded from patentability due to the lack of technical character. However, once they are expressed and claimed in terms of software/computer-implemented inventions (CIIs), they may have, in principle, the technical character required for patentability.

277. Inventions involving programs for computers can be protected[125] in different forms of 'computer-implemented inventions', or 'software-implemented inventions', or 'computer/software related inventions 'or simply 'software inventions' – expressions intended to cover claims which involve computers, computer networks or other programmable apparatus whereby at least one feature is realized by means of a program.

278. A computer program, claimed by itself, is not excluded from patentability if[126],[127] it is capable of bringing about, when running on or loaded into a computer, a further technical effect going beyond the 'normal' physical interactions between the program and the computer on which it is run.

279. On business methods, one can assert a similar approach, meaning that they are only excluded to the extent that the application and the claimed subject matter as this defines the matter for which protection is sought, relates to methods for doing business as such, but once the claimed method involves technical means, it does not relate to a method for doing business as such and its patentability is therefore not excluded.[128]

4. Presentations of Information

280. Similar to the previous cases, a pure feature relating to a presentation of information defined solely by the content of the information in whatever form and means does not have a technical character and accordingly, is excluded from patentability, but a technical means used for that presentation specifying one or more technical features and defining an apparatus in terms of its physical structure and

125. Strenc Alexandru –European Software Directives and European Software Patents. Pg. 115Wolters Kluwer 2017.
126. T 1173/97 OJ 1998.
127. G 3/08.
128. T 258/03, OJ 2004.

not in functional terms corresponding to the steps of that method, should be potentially patentable. In such cases, these examples show how a non-patentable presentation of information *as such,* receives the technical features necessary to overcome the exclusion from patentability.

C. Inventions Excepted form Patentability

281. EPC provides another category of inventions which, in spite of the fact that in principle they might meet the said patentability conditions, are simply excepted from patentability, by stipulating that :[129]

> European patents shall not be granted in respect of:
>
> (a) inventions the commercial exploitation of which would be contrary to 'ordre public' or morality; such exploitation shall not be deemed to be so contrary merely because it is prohibited by law or regulation in some or all of the Contracting States;
> (b) plant or animal varieties or essentially biological processes for the production of plants or animals; this provision shall not apply to microbiological processes or the products thereof;
> (c) methods for treatment of the human or animal body by surgery or therapy and diagnostic methods practiced on the human or animal body; this provision shall not apply to products, in particular substances or compositions, for use in any of these methods.

1. Inventions Contrary to Ordre Public or Morality

282. The concepts of ordre public or morality are not defined in the EPC; they are however dealt by the European case law which, referring to the first term, stipulated[130] that 'the concept of morality was related to the belief that some behaviour was right and acceptable whereas other behaviour was wrong, this belief being founded on the totality of the accepted norms which were deeply rooted in a particular culture'. The concept of 'ordre public' has been defined as[131] covering the protection of public security and the physical integrity of individuals as part of the society.

283. Most relevant cases arise mainly in connection with the sensitive question of biotechnological inventions, which led even to conflict situations in the EPO patenting practice- *see* patents for transgenic technology.

---

129. EPC Art. 53.
130. EPO Case Law of the Boards of Appeal IB 2.2.2.b; 8th Edition July 2016.
131. T 356/93.

284. In order to bring necessary clarifications, EPC provides that:[132]

> European patents shall not be granted in respect of biotechnological inventions[133] which, in particular, concern the following:
>
> (a) processes for cloning human beings;
> (b) processes for modifying the germ line genetic identity of human beings;
> (c) uses of human embryos for industrial or commercial purposes;
> (d) processes for modifying the genetic identity of animals which are likely to cause them suffering without any substantial medical benefit to man or animal, and also animals resulting from such processes.

The condition under point (d) focuses on three matters: animal suffering, medical benefit, and the necessary correspondence in terms of the animals in question and the case law considers that the test has to be applied to ensure that a patent extended only to those animals whose suffering was balanced by a medical benefit.[134]

2. Plant or Plant Varieties

285. Without further comments, we simply mention that the term 'plant variety' as defined in R. 26(4) EPC reproduces, in fact, the same definition as in Directive 98/44/EC on the legal protection of biotechnological inventions.

286. In applying Article 53(b) EPC,[135] a claim where the subject matter is directed to plant varieties is not patentable, however, if a product claim does not specify any particular plant variety but a technical teaching which can be embodied in an unspecified number of plant varieties, the subject matter of the claimed invention does not relate to a plant variety or varieties within the legal meaning and therefore should be patentable. Thus, a patent will not be granted for a single plant variety but can be granted if varieties may fall within the scope of the claims. If plant varieties are individually claimed, they are not patentable, irrespective of how they were made.[136]

287. Obtention of plants (and animals) as a result of biological processes is a clear barrier in their patenting as processes itself and as products obtained by these processes, as they lack technical character and EPC provides in this respect that 'European patents shall not be granted in respect of plants[137] ... exclusively obtained by means of an essentially biological process'.

132. EPC Art. 53(a).
133. EPC Rule 28(1).
134. T 315/03.
135. EPO Case Law of the Boards of Appeal I B 3.1; 8th Edition July 2016.
136. G 1/98, OJ 2000.
137. EPC Rule 28(2).

288. The EPO case law found that[138] ‘ the exception applying to “essentially biological processes for the production of plants” could not be read as limited to processes for the production of plant varieties because such an interpretation would be contrary to the wording’.

289. However, once the solution subject to patenting process proves to be technical (refers to a microbiological process), the process itself, and the plant and plant varieties obtained accordingly are patentable.

3. Animals or Animal Varieties

290. EPC case law[139] interpreted, in the same line, protection of animal and animal varieties by confirming the principle previously enunciated concerning plants and plant varieties, meaning that a patent could not be granted for a single animal variety (or species or race) but could be granted if varieties might fall within the scope of its claims.

291. Similar to plant protection, obtention of animals as a result of biological processes lacks technical character and consequently ‘European patents shall not be granted in respect of … animals[140] exclusively obtained by means of an essentially biological process’ but once the solution subject to patenting process proves to be technical (refers to a microbiological process), the process itself, and the animal and animal varieties obtained accordingly are patentable

4. Medical Methods

292. The two exceptions to patentability of the treatment and diagnostic methods appearing now in the new Article 53(c) EPC were attached among the inventions excluded to patentability.

293. Although this inclusion might appear as formal because the substantive reasons which laid the decision not to grant a patent for these types of methods remained the same, it appear as reasonable to exclude them from the activities where technical character is questioned, and rather to include them among the subject matters and activities where moral and ethical problems are concerned.

294. It is relevant in this respect, the fact that the EPO Enlarged Board of Appeal stated that the intention of Article 53(c) EPC was[141] to prevent non-commercial and non-industrial medical and veterinary activities from being restrained by patent

138. EPO Case Law of the Boards of Appeal IB 3.3.2 (a); 8th Edition July 2016.
139. T 315/03 OJ 2006.
140. EPC Rule 28(2).
141. G 1/83, G 5/83 and G 6/83 (OJ 1985, 60, 64, 67)- it is to be understood that the reference is however made to the old Art. 52(4) EPC 1973.

rights. Exclusion from patentability of the diagnostic methods is considered to be based on socio-ethical and public health considerations. [142] In a decision concerning treatment by surgery, the Enlarged Board considered that the mentioned exclusion had been deliberately maintained by the legislator, thereby[143] confirming the principle that medical and veterinary practitioners' necessity and freedom to apply the best available treatments to the benefit of their patients should be protected by excluding these activities from patentability.

295. It is considered that[144] 'the exclusions from patentability in Art. 53 EPC has been construed narrowly'.

296. However, according to the EPO case law, medical methods should not be analysed 'as a whole' and a clear distinction should be made in the approach towards methods for treatment by surgery or therapy on the one hand and diagnostic methods on the other.

297. Thus,[145] 'whilst a method claim falls under the prohibition on patenting methods for treatment by therapy or surgery if it comprises or encompasses at least one feature defining a physical activity or action that constitutes a method step for treatment of a human or animal body by surgery or therapy, a much narrower interpretation was applied with regard to the exclusion from patentability of diagnostic methods'.

298. By following a larger interpretation, the exclusion of surgery methods from patentability should not be applied[146] to methods in respect of which the interests of public health, of protection of patients, and as a counterpart, to that of the freedom of the medical profession to apply the treatment of choice to their patients does not call for their exclusion from patentability.

299. Similar surgical methods or therapeutic methods[147] cannot be patented if they include at least one feature defining physical activity or action that constitutes a method step for treatment of the human or animal body by therapy.

300. As mentioned, on diagnostic methods the EPO case law gave a narrow interpretation when stating that[148] in order for a claim relating to a diagnostic method practised on the human or animal body to fall under the prohibition of Article 52(4) EPC, that claim must include the features relating to:

(i) the diagnosis for curative purposes *stricto sensu* representing the deductive medical or veterinary decision phase as a purely intellectual exercise;

142. G 1/04 OJ 2006.
143. G 1/07 OJ 2011 and G 1/04 OJ 2006.
144. N. Fox A Guide to the EPC 2000, CIPA 2007, pg. 2.
145. EPO Case Law of the Boards of Appeal IB 4.2.1; 8th Edition July 2016.
146. G 1/07 OJ 2011.
147. EPO Case Law of the Boards of Appeal IB 4.4; 8th Edition July 2016.
148. G 1/04 OJ 2006.

(ii) the preceding steps which are constitutive for making that diagnosis, and
(iii) the specific interactions with the human or animal body which occur when carrying those out among these preceding steps which are of a technical nature.

II. Patentability Conditions

A. *Novelty*

301. An invention is considered to be new[149] 'if it does not form part of the state of the art. The state of the art shall be held to comprise everything made available to the public by means of a written or oral description, by use, or in any other way, before the date of filing of the European patent application'.

1. State of the Art and Absolute Novelty

302. The three attributes comprised in the definition of the state of the art, namely 'everything', 'anywhere' and by 'any means' reflects[150] the principle of absolute novelty, the state of the art comprising *everything* made available to the public *anywhere* in the world by means of a written or oral description, by use, or in *any other way*, before the date of filing or priority.

303. In the EPC, there is no definition for the concept of 'public', but its understanding focuses on 'more persons' once the case law[151] accepts that information is 'available to the public' if only a single member of the public is in a position to gain access to it and understand it. However, if the person who got the information on the invention was under a secrecy obligation, the invention cannot be considered to have been made available to the public, provided the person did not breach that obligation.

304. Article 54(3), constitutes prior art with effect for all the EPC Contracting States at the time of its publication, by including the content of European patent applications in the state of the art which were filed prior to the date of filing or priority of the examined patent application, but published on or after that date.

305. Applications having the same filing or priority date as the application to be examined are not part of the state of the art.[152]

306. It is to be noted that such earlier applications are part of the state of the art only when considering novelty and not when considering inventive step.

149. EPC Art. 54 Art. 54(1) and (2).
150. R. Schulte, Reiner Patentgesetzmit EPU 9 Auflage, 2007; pg.219.
151. T 1081/01, reason 5.
152. T 123/82.

307. Article 54(3) makes reference to the concept of 'content' of a European application, which refers to[153] 'the whole disclosure, i.e. the description, drawings, and claims, including:

(i) any matter explicitly disclaimed (with the exception of disclaimers for unworkable embodiments);
(ii) any matter for which an allowable reference to other documents is made; and
(iii) prior art insofar as explicitly described'.

308. The 'content' does not include, however, any priority document.

309. In assessing novelty, a prior document needs to be read and interpreted from the perspective of a person skilled in the art (*see* Chapter 3 §4 B 3) on its 'relevant date'. The relevant date of a prior document is its publication date, and that of a document within the meaning of Article 54(3) EPC is its date of filing (or, as the case may be, priority date).[154]

310. When assessing novelty, a document should not be interpreted using knowledge which only became available to the relevant experts between the publication date of the cited prior art and the filing or priority date of the application to be examined or the patent in dispute;[155] this is an issue which relates to inventive step.

2. Novelty of Medical Uses

311. Paragraphs 4 and 5 of Article 54 regulate, in fact, the patentability of the so-called first medical use when provided, is not excluded:

> the patentability of any substance or composition, comprised in the state of the art, for use in a method referred to in Article 53(c) (e.g. methods for treatment of the human or animal body by surgery or therapy and diagnostic methods practiced on the human or animal body), provided that its use for any such method is not comprised in the state of the art

and respectively 'second and further medical uses' when provided, is not excluded

> the patentability of any substance or composition referred to in paragraph 4 for any specific use in a method referred … provided that such use is not comprised in the state of the art.

---

153. EPO Guidelines for Examination G IV, 5.1; November 2017.
154. EPO Guidelines for Examination G–VI, 3; November 2015.
155. T 205/91.

312. First provision relate to what is known as a 'first medical indication of a per se already known substance or composition'[156] by which[157] 'in addition to the general concept of novelty, this article introduces, in respect of substances and compounds used in surgical and therapeutic treatment and in diagnostic processes carried out on humans and animals, a special concept of novelty unknown in other technical fields'.

313. This type of invention is usually protected by a purpose-related product type of claim.

314. New Article 54(5) EPC eliminates any possible legal uncertainty on the patentability of further medical use when it permits purpose-related product protection for each new further medical use of a substance or composition already known as a medicine.

315. Based on a decision of the Enlarged Board,[158] EPO however allowed, even before the EPC 2000, protection of a claim directed to the use of a substance or composition for the manufacture of a medicament for a specified therapeutic application, formulated as the so-called Swiss-type claim. But once this new provision was enforced, it unambiguously allowed a normal protection of purpose-related product protection for each further new medical use of a substance or composition already known as a medicine and claims to a second medical use would be drafted as product claims relating to a specific second or further medical use.[159]

316. To conclude on EPC approach on the novelty (patentability) of inventions in medical field, according to Article 53 (c), patents cannot be granted for methods of treatment or diagnosis but however, may be obtained for new products, particularly, substances or compositions for use in these methods of treatment or diagnosis.

317. Where the substance or composition is known, according to Article 54(4) it may only be patented for use in these methods if the known substance or composition was not previously disclosed for use in medical methods practised on the human or animal body ('first medical use'). If the known substance or composition was previously disclosed for use in a first medical method practised on the human or animal body a 'further medical use', maybe however claimed for the new specific medical use.

318. It is considered that[160] 'putting the first medical use on a par with each further medical use in terms of novelty does not have to affect the scope of the claims for the first medical use'.

---

156. G 2/08, OJ 2010.
157. T 128/82, OJ 1984.
158. G 5/83 OJ 1985.
159. T 1599/06.
160. EPO CA/PL 25/00 Rev. 1; Basic Proposal for the Revision of the European Patent Convention; Munich, 28.07.2000.

3. Non-prejudicial Disclosure Versus 'Grace Period'

319. A specific discussion deserves the 'non-prejudicial disclosure', where European law and practice present significant differences comparing with those in the US and most other industrialized countries, where it is rather considered as a 'grace period' based on distinct presumptions, provisions, and implementation. Thus, according to the EPC [161] a disclosure of the invention shall not be taken into consideration if it occurred no earlier than six months preceding the filing of the European patent application and if it was due to, or in consequence of, an evident abuse in relation to the applicant or his legal predecessor, or based on the fact that the applicant or his legal predecessor has displayed the invention at an official, or officially recognized, international exhibition.

320. In this case, the applicant has to state, when filing the European patent application, that the invention has been so displayed and file a supporting certificate within the prescribed time limits and conditions. However, if the applicant failed to file a certificate in due time, the loss of right can be still avoided[162] if the said certificate is filed, with payment of due fees, within the next two months of notification of loss of rights.

321. For the calculation of the six-month period, the relevant date[163] to refer is the date of the current filing of the European patent application; the date of priority is not to be taken account of in calculating this period. It is therefore irrelevant that a European patent application claims priority from an earlier application which has been currently within the prescribed six-month period.

322. The non-prejudicial disclosure makes reference to two specific concepts that need our attention. The first one is 'evident abuse', which is not regulated under the EPC and rest to the courts to deal with it. It is considered that in order to be concluded, there must be, from the person disclosing the invention, either current intent to cause harm or current or constructive knowledge that harm would or could ensue from this disclosure.[164]

323. The second item concerns official, or officially recognized, international exhibition, and for clarification, their list is published in the Official Journal and should fall, according to Article 52(2) EPC, within the terms of the convention on international exhibitions signed at Paris on 22 November 1928 and last revised on 30 November 1972

161. EPC Art. 55.
162. EPC Art. 121; rule 135.
163. G 3/98; G2/99.
164. T585/92.

324. Contrary to the non-prejudicial disclosure, the grace period is a period of time prior to the filing or priority date of a patent application, during which an inventor can freely divulge his invention without it destroying the novelty of his invention for patenting purposes.

325. There are many ways in which a grace period can be defined, and consequently, the international landscape in this respect is a patchwork of different regimes.[165]

326. A common approach is to have a twelve months period, where a disclosure made usually by professors and/or researchers is not prejudicial if within this period a patent application for the disclosed invention is filed with the Patent Office.

327. It is not our intention to detail a concept which in fact is not applicable in Europe, but however, it is to be mentioned that intense discussion took place under various forums which included European officials[166] for a harmonized approach on grace period.

328. Two points of convergence might indicate a possible agreement in the future.

329. First, the grace period must be a 'safety-net' grace period, which would reduce the consequences of accidental disclosure, allow early academic publication and simultaneously limit legal uncertainty. A safety-net grace period would be defined by the following features:

Duration: at most six months, calculated from the priority date.

Mandatory declaration requirement: mandatory list of disclosures specifying when, how and which information about the invention was made available to the public.

- Prior user rights: a third party acting in good faith should have the right to continue using an invention, provided such use or serious and effective preparations to use the invention began before the filing or priority date of the patent application.
- Protection from disclosure of independent inventions: the grace period would only apply to disclosures of the applicant's invention, and not to independent disclosures made by third parties.

330. Second, the grace period must be internationally harmonized in the key global patent systems including, besides Europe, at least the US, Japan, Korea and

165. Workshop Report The Economic Effects of Introducing a Grace Period in Europe; EPO Economic and Scientific Advisory Board Munich, 26 Nov. 2014.
166. Negociations on SPLT Substantive Patent Law Treaty; Bodensee Group, etc.

China, and possibly India and Brazil. This is in the interest of any entities contemplating patenting in multiple jurisdictions.

4. Basic Consideration in Assessing Novelty

331. The jurisprudence and practice of the EPO developed some basic principles when assessing and judging novelty.

332. The EPO's practice in examining general condition of novelty requires the so-called 1:1 comparison, where it is considered to be fulfilled if the solution in the invention differentiates with at least one technical characteristic from the closest state of the art.[167]

333. Novelty is prejudiced[168] only by something which is clearly disclosed to a skilled person in a *single* source of prior art, for example, in a patent application published before the date of priority. The claimed invention lacks novelty only if a 'clear and unmistakable teaching' of a combination of the claimed features could be found in a prior art disclosure.[169]

334. Novelty is generally assessed if not all features of a claim are known from a single item of prior art. It is not permissible to combine separate items of prior art together neither to combine separate items belonging to different embodiments described in one and the same document unless such combination has specifically been suggested[170]

335. A specific requirement for the assessing the novelty, especially for inventions in chemistry, is that[171] a generic disclosure does not usually take away the novelty of any specific example falling within the terms of that disclosure, but that a specific disclosure does take away the novelty of a generic claim embracing that disclosure.

336. EPO patenting practice is based on a narrow concept of novelty where the content of a prior publication must be interpreted narrowly,[172] an interpretation which excludes the taking into account of equivalents of the features which are explicitly or implicitly disclosed in the disclosure of a prior document, contrary equivalents being considered only when assessing inventive step.[173]

167. J. Strauss Deutsches und Europeisches Patentrecht, Max Planck 2001.
168. EPO Guide for applicants: How to Get a European patent, B II, July 2017 (17th edition).
169. T 450/89.
170. T 305/87.
171. EPO Guidelines for Examination G VI, 5; November 2017.
172. T 447/92.
173. T 517/90.

B. Inventive Step

337. EPC provides that an invention shall be considered as involving an inventive step if,[174] 'having regard to the state of the art, it is not obvious to a person skilled in the art'.

338. Contrary to the assessment of novelty, where the state of the art also includes the content of European patent applications filed prior to the date of filing or priority of the examined patent application, but which were published on or after that date, EPC provides that for the assessment of inventive step, these documents are not to be considered.

1. Problem Solution Approach

339. In trying to find the most adequate way and means to maximise the objectivity of assessing this fundamental patentability condition, the EPO's practice in examining and deciding whether or not claimed subject matter fulfils the requirements of inventive step is extensively based, from a certain number of years, on the so-called problem and solution approach. This consists essentially of :[175]

(a) identifying the 'closest prior art';
(b) assessing the technical results (or effects) achieved by the claimed invention when compared with the 'closest state of the art' established;
(c) defining the 'objective technical problem' to be solved as the object of the invention to achieve these results; and
(d) examining whether or not a skilled person, having regard to the closest state of the art, would have suggested the claimed technical features in order to obtain the results achieved by the claimed invention

340. Problem and solution are component parts of any technical invention and this arises from the EPC provisions according to which[176] the invention, as claimed, must be disclosed 'in such terms that the technical problem, even if not expressly stated as such, and its solution can be understood and state any advantageous effects of the invention with reference to the background art'.

341. The problem and solution approach is not mandatory in the EPO practice,[177] but its correct application facilitates the objective assessment of inventive step and therefore it is highly encouraged because it is considered that the EPO practice aims at ensuring an objective assessment of inventive step and avoid ex post facto analysis of the prior art

174. EPC Art. 56.
175. EPO Guidelines for Examination G–VII, 5; November 2017.
176. EPC Rule 42(1) c.
177. EPO -Case Law of the Boards of Appeal I D 2; November 2015.

342. The concept of the 'closest prior art' for assessing inventive step is not defined in the EPC, but the EPO patenting practice considers it [178] 'a prior art document disclosing subject matter conceived for the same purpose or aiming at the same objective as the claimed invention and having the most relevant technical features in common, i.e. requiring the minimum of structural modifications'.

343. A further criterion for the selection of the most promising starting point is the similarity of technical problems.

344. The closest prior art is, therefore, an objective concept made based on an objective comparison of the subject matter, objectives and features of the various items of prior art leading to the identification of one such item as the closest.[179]

345. In the context of the problem and solution approach, the 'objective technical problem' is defined as a technical problem having the aim and task of modifying or adapting the closest prior art to provide the technical effects that the invention provides over the closest prior art.

346. This presupposes that the claimed invention must be examined whether the problem, defined by reference to the closest prior art, has indeed been solved. If not, the problem must be reformulated in order to become 'objective'.

2. Could-Would Test

347. To determine whether the claimed invention, starting from the closest prior art and based on the technical problem as has been objectively determined by problem and solution approach, would have been obvious to the skilled person, the EPO and its boards are currently applying the so-called *could-would test.* This implies estimating not whether the skilled person *could* have carried out the invention, but rather, whether he *would have done* so in its activity of giving the solution to the underlying technical problem raised by that invention.

348. The EPO case law starts from the presumption that when assessing if the claimed subject matter constitutes an obvious solution to an objective technical problem, the question is if the skilled person, in the expectation of solving the problem, would have modified the teaching in the closest prior art document in the light of other teachings in the prior art so as to arrive at the claimed invention[180] and accordingly, the point is not whether the skilled person could have arrived at the invention by modifying the prior art, but rather, whether in expectation of the advantages currently achieved (i.e., in the light of the technical problem addressed), he would have done it based on the prior art.[181]

178. EPO -Case Law of the Boards of Appeal I D3.1; November 2015.
179. T 1212/01.
180. T 1014/07.
181. T 219/87.

349. When assessing inventive step, the dangerous conclusions of an ex post facto approach should be carefully avoided,[182] which might be easily taken into consideration, especially for inventions which at first sight seem obvious, for combination inventions, and where the proposed solution is supposedly 'simple'.

350. From a legal point of view, this implies that the inventive step of the proposed invention should be assessed by taking into account the technical landscape of the *ante facto* state of the art valid by the priority date, and not that as perceived by a person skilled in the art by the time of examination.

3. Invention Obvious to a Person Skilled in the Art

351. The EPC is silent on legal definitions for the terms 'obvious' and 'person skilled in the art'. So, it has been left to the practice of the EPO and the jurisprudence of the Boards of Appeal, and of course to the relevant doctrine, to offer guidance in their respect.

352. According to the case law of the Boards of Appeal, the person skilled in the art should be presumed to be[183] an experienced practitioner who has average knowledge and abilities and is aware of what was common general knowledge in the relevant art concerned at a particular time, or in other words, could be regarded as an average skilled person. He should also be presumed to have had access to everything in the state of the art, in particular, the documents cited in the search report, and to have had at his disposal the normal means and capacity for routine work and experimentation. The skilled person will be an expert in a technical field,[184] namely in the technical field where the technical solution is given to the technical problem posed by that invention.

353. The term 'obvious' means[185] that which does not go beyond the normal progress of technology but merely follows plainly or logically from the prior art, that is, something which does not involve the exercise of any skill or ability beyond that to be expected of the person skilled in the art.

354. As previously mentioned under subsection *A*, the concept/doctrine of equivalents is recognized in the EPO's practice as specific for the assessment of inventive step but not for novelty. On this concept, the EPO case law considers that[186] two means are equivalent if, despite having different embodiments, they are fulfilling the same function with regard to the same result.

---

182. EPO Guidelines dor Examination G–VII, 3; November 2017.
183. *Ibid.*
184. T 641/00, OJ 2003.
185. EPO Guidelines for Examination G VII 4 November 2017.
186. T 697/92.

355. A specific discussion on inventive step is required for 'computer/software-implemented inventions' where the technicality of the invention is a sensitive and difficult-to-solve question.[187]

356. In order to meet the patentability condition of inventive step, the CII must make a non-obvious technical contribution that is to bring a contribution to the state of the art in a technical field which is not obvious to a person skilled in the art, by a non-obvious solution to a technical problem defined in terms of technical features.

357. This is to be regarded as a qualification of, and not a substitute for, the definition of inventive step as provided in Article 56 of the EPC.

358. Thus, a CII in which the contribution to the prior art does not have a technical character does not satisfy the patentability condition of inventive step.

359. This assertion is true even if the non-technical contribution to the prior art is not obvious. When assessing inventive step, the questions as to what is to be included in the state of the art and the knowledge of the skilled person must be determined according to the criteria applied when assessing inventive step in general.

4. Secondary Indicia of Inventive Step

360. With the same aim of finding an objective evaluation of the prior art teachings in assessing inventive step, the need to provide a clearer picture on the evaluation has been considered by EPO patenting practice for a number of the so-called secondary indicia or circumstantial indicia of inventive step, namely:[188]

– Predictable disadvantage; non-functional modification; arbitrary choice.
– Unexpected technical effect; bonus effect.
– Long-felt need; commercial success.

as well as some other:

– Age of documents – time factor.
– Satisfaction of a long-felt need.
– Market competitors.
– Simple solution.
– Comparative tests.

187. Strenc Alexandru Cristian –European Sofware Directives and European Sofware Patents. pg. 130, Wolters Kluwer 2017.

188. EPO Guidelines for Examination G VII 10 Nov. 2017.

361. It is considered that[189] 'these indicia are however merely auxiliary considerations in the assessment of inventive step and no substitute for the problem and solution approach. The secondary indicia are a ragbag of arguments in favor or against inventive step that carry different weight'. They have their importance, especially in cases of doubt, when a clearer picture is supplementarily needed in the objective evaluation of the prior art teachings.

C. Industrial Application

362. EPC provides that[190] 'an invention shall be considered as susceptible of industrial application if it can be made or used in any kind of industry, including agriculture'.

363. This patentability condition does not imply currently achieving the industrial application of a product or a process but rather indicates the susceptibility or possibility of it and thus, clearly indicating sufficient possibility of making or using the invention in any kind of industry. [191] Agriculture is also a kind of industry for the purposes of the EPC.[192]

364. It is also important to note that the legal provision indicates an alternative condition that invention 'can be made *or* used' and not the concomitant one 'made *and* used', which has a direct practical implication.

365. From a practical point of view, an invention is considered as industrially applicable if 'the nature of the invention is suitable either to be produced in a technical undertaking or to have a technical use in a technical undertaking'. [193]

366. The description should indicate[194] explicitly, the way in which the invention is 'capable of exploitation in the industry' if this is not obvious from the description or from the nature of the invention; this means, in fact, the same as 'susceptible of industrial application'. It is therefore 'to be expected that, in most cases, the way in which the invention can be exploited in the industry will be self-evident, so that no more explicit description on this point will be required'.

367. Another requirement for an invention to be considered susceptible of industrial application is[195] that the technical teaching disclosed in the application is reproducible.

---

189. Bardhele Pagenberg - Assessment of Inventive Step under the EPC; www.bardehle.com.
190. EPC Art. 57.
191. T 144/83.
192. T 116/85, OJ 1989.
193. R. Schulte Patentgesetz mit EPU 9 Auflage, 2007, pg. 292.
194. EPO Guidelines for Examination F–II,4.9; November 2017 version.
195. EPO Case Law of the Boards of Appeal; I E 2; 8th edition, July 2016.

368. The board held that[196] reproducibility was to be assessed in the first instance when stating that the invention must be disclosed in such a way that it can be carried out by a skilled person. Thus, it has been considered[197] ' that Art. 57 could also serve as a basis for objecting to a lack of reproducibility because an invention that could not be carried out was also not susceptible of industrial application'.

369. The EPO patenting practice considers that[198] 'the industrial applicability requirement might play a decisive role in the determination of the patentability in respect of three types of inventions:

(a) those which appear to be impossible to carry out because they contravene the laws of physics (for example, a perpetual motion machine);
(b) those concerning methods which could be considered to fall entirely within the private or personal sphere;
(c) those involving gene sequences, for which the industrial application must be disclosed.'

370. Usually, industrial applicability should result from the description of the claimed invention but it must be indicated explicitly, 'when it is not obvious from the description or nature of the invention, the way in which the invention is industrially applicable'.[199] However, this explicit indication must be performed in the field of biotechnological inventions where EPC provides that the industrial application of a sequence or a partial sequence of a gene must be disclosed in the patent application.[200]

III. Persons Entitled to a European Patent

371. European patent application may be filed by any natural or legal person, or anybody equivalent to a legal person by virtue of the law governing it.[201] They may also be filed either by joint applicants or by two or more applicants designating different Contracting States.[202]

372. A breakdown by category of applicants requesting services from the EPO shows[203] that 66% of them were large companies, 28% were SMEs and individual inventors, and 6% were universities and public research institutes. This shows that in spite of the fact that European patents are by their nature, area of effect, and costs,

196. T 718/96.
197. *Ibid.*
198. WIPO SCP/9/5 March 17, 2003-E 'industrial applicability' and 'utility' requirements: Commonalities and differences.
199. EPC Regulation Rule 42(1)(f).
200. EPC Regulation Rule 29(3).
201. EPC Art. 58.
202. EPC Art. 59.
203. EPO-Annual report 2016.

mostly filed by big companies, nevertheless a significant proportion of applicants at the EPO are smaller entities. The percentage of 6% for universities and public research institutes is probably smaller than desired and Europe should indeed look for a better situation compared to US, Japan, or South Korea.

373. In 2016, European patent filings grew again (+6.2%), reaching a new high of more than 296,000 applications.

374. The EPO received nearly 160,000 European patent applications in 2016, nearly at the same level as the record number reached the year before. The total applications included nearly 95,000 international PCT filings which entered the European regional phase (becoming European applications) in 2016, and some 65,000 European patent applications filed directly at the EPO under the EPC.

375. Regarding relevant EPO statistics on biggest patent applicants, they appear, in general, as good for Europe. Thus, a big European company filed the most patent applications at the EPO in 2016 the second year in a row and in the top 10 entered four companies from Europe, three from the US, two from South Korea and one from China

376. In line with basic international principles and patent laws, EPC provides that the right to a European patent[204] shall belong to the inventor or his successor in title and in case when two or more persons have made an invention independently of each other, the right belongs to the person whose European patent application has the earliest date of filing, subject to condition that it has been published.

377. The rights, in case of employee's inventions, is left to the national patent law of the state in which the employee is mainly employed, or if that state cannot be determined, the applicable is that of the state in which the employer has the place of business to which the employee is attached.

378. Until the contrary, in all patenting procedures before the EPO, the applicant is considered to have the right to a European patent and this fiction only allows the EPO to perform no investigation on the existence of the entitlement.

379. However, when another person than the applicant disputes the entitlement to the grant of a European patent, the entitlement may be modified whereby a final decision it is adjudged that another person is entitled to the grant of the European patent, and in these circumstances, that person may:[205]

- prosecute the European patent application as his own application in place of the original applicant;
- file a new European patent application in respect of the same invention; or
- request that the European patent application be refused.

204. EPC Art. 60.
205. EPC Art. 61.

380. The EPO case law held[206] that when it has been adjudged by a final decision of a national court that a person other than the applicant is entitled to the grant of a European patent and that person files, under relevant EPC provision, a new European patent application in respect of the same invention, 'it is not a precondition for the application to be accepted that the earlier original usurping application is still pending before the EPO at the time the new application is filed'.

381. On remedies, as provided in Article 61 EPC, reference could be found in the Protocol on Jurisdiction (*see* Chapter 4 §3) which determines where entitlement proceedings may be brought when a European patent application is alleged to have been filed by a person who is not entitled.

382. EPC provides[207] the right of the inventor to be mentioned in the patent application and specification unless[208] he informs the EPO in writing that he has waived his right to be thus mentioned.

IV. Effects of the European Patent and the European Patent Application

A. *Term of Protection*

383. The maximum term of a European patent is[209] twenty years from the date of filing of the application. However, the patent may lapse earlier if the annual renewal fees are not paid or if the patent is revoked by the patentee or after opposition proceedings.

384. In certain cases, the EPC provides nevertheless two situations for the right of a Contracting State to extend the term of a European patent, or to grant corresponding protection which follows immediately on expiry of the term of the patent, under the same conditions as those applying to national patents, namely:

– national emergency conditions affecting that state;
– if the subject matter of the European patent is a product or a process for manufacturing a product or a use of a product which has to undergo an administrative authorization procedure required by law before it can be put on the market in that state, and in particular it is about supplementary protection certificates for medicinal and phytopharmaceuticals which are extending the period of protection[210]

206. EPO-Case Law of the Boards of Appeal; IV A 4; 8th edition, July 2016.
207. EPC Art. 62.
208. EPC Rule 20.
209. EPC Art. 63.
210. Council Regulation (EEC) No 1768/92 concerning the creation of a supplementary protection certificate for medicinal products (codified as Regulation (EC) no 469/2009 of the European Parliament and of the Council of 6 May 2009 concerning the supplementary protection certificate for medicinal products) and Regulation (EC) No 1610/96 of the European Parliament and of the Council concerning the creation of a supplementary protection certificate for plant protection products.

385. A Contracting State which makes provision for the mentioned extension of the term or corresponding protection may, in accordance with an agreement, entrust to the EPO tasks associated with implementation of the relevant provisions.

386. European patents confer[211] on its proprietor from the date on which the mention of their grant is published in the European Patent Bulletin in each Contracting State in respect of which it is granted, the same rights as would be conferred by a national patent granted in that state.

387. EPC provides the so-called extension of the protection conferred by the process patents extend to the products directly obtained by such processes, extremely important in particular in chemical and pharma industry.

388. Due to the legal transformation of a European patent once granted by the EPO in a bundle of national patents, if the validation process is accomplished for the concerned states, EPC provides in the same Article that 'any infringement of a European patent shall be dealt with by national law'.

B. Translation of the European Patent

389. For the of the EPC Contracting States which have at least one official language different from English, French, or German, the national validation process needs a translation in that (those) language(s) under provided conditions[212] that will also be further commented.

390. Thus, the concerned Contracting State may, if the European patent as granted, amended, or limited by the EPO is not drawn up in one of its official languages, prescribe that the proprietor of the patent shall supply to its NPO a translation of the patent as granted, amended, or limited in one of its official languages at his option or, where that state has prescribed the use of one specific official language, in that language. As a general rule, translation must be filed, within three months after the date on which the mention of the grant, maintenance in amended form, or limitation of the European patent is published in the European Patent Bulletin. Failure to observe the provided time limit leads to the legal situation that the European patent is deemed to be void *ab initio* in that state.

391. The London Agreement on the application of Article 65 (*see* Chapter 5 & 2) provides for the EPC Contracting States which ratified it, a gradual dispensing policy with the translation requirements as provided in the related article.

211. EPC Art. 64.
212. EPC Art. 65.

392. Under Article 1(1) of the London Agreement, a Contracting State to the agreement which has an official language in common with one of the official languages of the EPO will dispense with the translation requirements under Article 65(1) EPC.

393. An overall situation on translation requirements in the EPC Contracting States[213] is as follows:

> 17 Contracting States to the EPC, namely: Austria, Belgium, Bulgaria, Cyprus, the Czech Republic, Estonia, Greece, Italy, Malta, Poland, Portugal, Romania, San Marino, Serbia, Slovakia, Spain and Turkey, have enacted provisions under Article 65 (1) and (2) EPC and they require a full translation of the patent specification.
>
> 21 Contracting States have ratified the London Agreement (Albania, Croatia, Denmark, Finland, the former Yugoslav Republic of Macedonia, France, Germany, Hungary, Iceland, Ireland, Latvia, Lithuania, Liechtenstein, Luxembourg, Monaco, the Netherlands, Norway, Slovenia, Sweden, Switzerland and the UK) and by that these states agreed to dispense entirely or partly with the translation requirements.

394. Among these, eight Contracting States have an official language in common with at least one the official language of the EPO, namely France, Germany, Ireland, Liechtenstein, Luxembourg, Monaco, Switzerland, and the UK and accordingly, they agreed to dispense entirely with the translation requirements.

395. The other remaining states, namely Albania, Croatia, Denmark, Finland, Hungary, Iceland, the Netherlands, Norway, and Sweden do not have an official language in common with the EPO and consequently they require a translation of the claims to be filed in one of their official languages if the European patent has been granted in English, or has been translated into English and filed under Article 65(1) EPC. Except for Croatia, the European patent specification can also be filed in these countries in the respective country's language. The former Yugoslav Republic of Macedonia, Latvia, Lithuania, and Slovenia only require a translation of the claims into their respective official languages regardless of the official language in which the EPO has granted the patent. All EPC Contracting States have implemented in their national law, the provision of Article 65(3) EPC that failure to observe the prescribed time limit, the European patent will be deemed to be void *ab initio*. It is also a matter of the national law of the Contracting States concerned to regulate circumstances of such a loss of rights, the time limit for filing the translation being at a large scale non-extendable.

396. Based on the effect of the European patent as a national patent and the dispense of the translation requirements, the proprietor needs to take no action of validation before the NPO in France, Germany, Ireland, Luxembourg, Monaco,

---

213. EPO- National Law Relating to the EPC; 18th edition, October 2017.

Switzerland/Liechtenstein, or the UK and subject to the condition that no revocation or limitation of the European patent occurred, the said patent takes effect as a national patent on the date on which the mention of the grant is published in the European Patent Bulletin.

397. If the European patent application contains different sets of claims for different states, due to different claims of priorities originating from different Contracting States,[214] it is requested that only a translation of the set of claims applicable to the state in question be filed.

C. Effects of a European Patent Application

398. EPC provides three major effects of a European patent application once they got a date of filing.

399. The first one is based on its equivalence with a regular national, filing meaning that

> A European patent application which has been accorded a date of filing shall, in the designated Contracting States, be equivalent to a regular national filing, where appropriate with the priority claimed for the European patent application.[215]

400. The second one refers to the provisional protection conferred by a European patent application after publication[216] and consequently, it provisionally offers such protection as conferred by Article 64 EPC in the Contracting States designated in the application as published, that is, the same rights as would be conferred by a national patent granted in those states.

401. The second paragraph provides the freedom of the Contracting States to prescribe that a European patent application does not confer the protection referred to above. The protection attached to the publication of the European patent application may not, however, be less than that which would result from publication of an unexamined national patent application. The applicant must at least be given the right to claim reasonable compensation in the circumstances from an unauthorized user.

402. A further exception to the basic rule refers to the date from which provisional protection is effective for any Contracting State which does not have, as an official language, the language of the proceedings, that Contracting State being free to prescribe that provisional protection is to be effective until such time as a translation of the claims in one of its official languages at the option of the applicant or,

214. EPC Rule 138.
215. EPC Art. 66.
216. EPC Art. 67.

where that state has prescribed the use of one specific official language, in that language, has been made available to the public in the manner prescribed by national law or has been communicated to the person using the invention in the said state.

403. No time limits are prescribed for filing the above-mentioned translations in the Contracting States; provisional protection in the individual Contracting States becomes effective only when the conditions previously referred to translation, have been fulfilled.

404. However, the European patent application does not offer the benefit of provisional protection when it has been withdrawn, deemed to be withdrawn, or finally refused. The same applies in respect to the effects of the European patent application in a Contracting State the designation of which is withdrawn or deemed to be withdrawn.

405. The third effect is a direct consequence of the revocation or limitation of the European patent[217] made in the opposition, limitation, or revocation proceedings, according to which the European patent application and the resulting European patent are deemed not to offer, from the outset, the benefit of provided protection.

406. The wording of Article 68 is the result of the revised EPC 2000 and incorporates limitation proceedings (*see* Article 105a–c) and national revocation proceedings into the provisions governing opposition proceedings, whereby the European patent is deemed not to have had effect, as from the outset, to the extent that the patent has been revoked or limited.

407. It thus[218] uniformly establishes the retroactive effect of limiting or revoking a European patent in opposition, limitation and (national) revocation proceedings. The inclusion of national revocation proceedings reflects the fact that the revocation of European patents now has an ex tunc effect in all Contracting States, and it formalises the harmonization achieved in that respect.

V. Extent of Protection

408. This concept is covered by Article 69 EPC and its Protocol of interpretation (*see* Chapter 4 §6) according to which, the extent of the protection conferred by a European patent or a European patent application shall be determined by the claims, but the said texts indicate two ways of having a full interpretation of their wording. The first one is offered by the article itself when providing that the description and drawings shall be used to interpret the claims; and the other one, offered by

217. EPC Art. 68.
218. EPO CA/PL 25/00 Rev. 1; Basic Proposal for the Revision of the European Patent Convention; Munich, 28.07.2000.

the Protocol, which pledges for a balanced approach between a strict, literal meaning of the wording used in the claims, and contrarily, a guideline of what the patent proprietor has contemplated.

409. Between the moment when the patent application is published and the European patent is granted, the extent of the provisional protection conferred by the European patent application is determined by the claims contained in the published application but once the European patent was granted or amended in opposition, limitation, or revocation proceedings, its granted claims determine retroactively, the protection conferred by the application in so far as such protection is not thereby extended.

410. In this respect, interpretation of Article 69 EPC must always be reflected in the provisions of Article 123(3) which stipulates that:

> the European patent may not be amended in such a way as to extend the protection it confers.

411. The EPO case law holds that[219] interpreting the extent of protection was a matter for national courts dealing with infringement cases and the EPO itself is concerned in opposition appeal proceedings with the extent of protection conferred by a patent only for the purposes of examining compliance with Article 123(3) EPC and nothing beyond that.

412. It considers the assumption that the extent of protection referred to in Article 123(3) EPC depends not only on the current wording of the claims but also on their validity in view of the prior art and has no support from the provisions of Article 69 EPC.[220]

413. There are indeed (at least) two situations where the interpretation of the claims by the content of the description is needed, namely where the claims are in need of interpretation, for example, because of functional or unclear features, or where a well known and generally accepted meaning of a term is overthrown and replaced by a new definition given in the description.

414. In this respect, it was held that [221] the use of the description and drawings to interpret the claims does not apply to cases where an unambiguous and generally accepted definition of a term figuring in the claims is to be superseded by a different definition found in the description. If it was intended that a term which was in no need of any interpretation be given a new meaning, then the definition for this new meaning had to be put into the claims.

---

219. EPO Case Law of the Boards of Appeal; IIA 6.3.6; 8th Edition July 2016.
220. T 325/95.
221. T 177/08.

415. It is important to recall that the interpretation of the claims belongs to the skilled person who, when considering a claim, should rule out interpretations which are illogical or which do not make technical sense.[222]

416. Accordingly, the scope of protection should not be interpreted, however, in the light of the intention of the drafter of a claim, since this was a subjective criterion, but rather on the basis of the meaning generally accepted by the person skilled in the art to the technical features defined in the said claim.[223]

417. It is indeed of a paramount importance for a real and effective enforcement of the protection conferred by both the application and related patent granted, the provision of the EPC stating which is considered the authentic text of a European patent application or European patent. Several situations are regulated namely:

- in proceedings before the EPO and in any Contracting State, the authentic text is the text of the application or of the related patent in the language of the proceedings;
- if however, the European patent application has been filed in a different language of one of the official languages of the EPO, the text of the application as filed is the authentic text;
- the Contracting States have the freedom to provide that a translation into one of its official languages, is to be regarded as authentic, except for revocation proceedings, in the event of the European patent application or European patent in the language of the translation conferring protection which is narrower than that conferred by it in the language of the proceedings. In this situation, that Contracting State:
  - must allow the applicant for or proprietor of the patent to file a corrected translation of the European patent application or European patent;
  - may prescribe that any person who, in that state, in good faith has used or has made effective and serious preparations for using an invention the use of which would not constitute an infringement of the application or patent in the original translation, may, after the corrected translation takes effect, continue such use.

VI. The European Patent Application as an Object of Property

418. EPC provides explicitly that the pending patent applications filed with the EPO, considered as objects of property, may be transferred by assignment or licensing or give rise to rights for one or more of the designated Contracting States.[224]

222. T 190/99.
223. T 999/10.
224. EPC Art. 71.

419. Assignments must be made in writing under the signature of the parties to the contract.[225]

420. Contractual licensing[226] may cover licences with effect in whole or in part for the whole or part of the territories of the designated Contracting States. The recordal of exclusive licences and sub-licences are expressly permitted at the EPO[227] and also recordal of licences can be cancelled on request[228]

421. According to the EPC, the applicable law [229] in each designated Contracting State and with effect for such state for the transfer of rights if the European patent application is the national law of the state concerned as valid for national patent applications. However, it should be noted that a centralized procedure for recordal of the licences and other rights is only permitted at the EPO during the processing of the patent application but after granting the related patent, central recordal is no more possible and from there onwards, they are under national law of the state where the patent is valid.

§5. Grant Procedure

I. Filing of a European Patent Application

422. A European patent application may be filed[230] with the EPO, or according to the law of a Contracting State, with the central industrial property office or other competent authority of that state and the application filed in this way has the same effect as if it had been filed on the same date with the EPO. Consequently, European patent applications may be filed[231] at the EPO at Munich, its branch at The Hague, its sub-office in Berlin (however not in Vienna) or, if the law of a Contracting State so permits, at the central industrial property office or other competent authority of that state.

423. EPC provides the possibility of implementing specific national legislation on inventions which, due to the nature of their subject matter, may not be communicated abroad without a prior internal authorization or which are prescribed that related applications must be filed initially with a national authority or directly filed with another authority but subject to prior authorization.

424. In all cases, the central industrial property office of the concerned Contracting State must forward to the EPO any European patent application filed with

225. EPC Art. 72.
226. EPC Art. 73.
227. EPC Rule 24.
228. EPC Rule 23.
229. EPC Art. 73.
230. EPC Art. 75.
231. National law relating to the EPC (September 2015, 17th edition); pg. 69.

it or any other competent authority in that state,[232] excepting the European patent applications, the subject of which has been made secret which shall not be forwarded.

425. The consequence in case a European patent application is not forwarded to the EPO in due time shall be deemed to be withdrawn.

426. For the purpose of filing an application, a national representative does not need to be appointed if the applicant has neither a residence nor his principal place of business within the territory of the state concerned.[233]

427. A translation in respect of every application which is not in English, French, or German must be filed in one of these languages within two months of filing the European application,[234] subject to the condition that if this translation is not filed in due time, the application is deemed to be withdrawn.

428. With regard to the languages of the applications, applicants are recommended to file applications where possible in the official language(s) of these states as difficulties in communication may arise. For instance, in most of the states, the applications are under the obligation of national security regulations, where imposing specific time limits of which non-observance of forwarding such applications might lead to situations where European patent applications are deemed to be withdrawn.

429. European divisional application must always be filed directly with the EPO,[235] that is, at Munich, The Hague, or Berlin and must cover only the subject matter which does not extend beyond the content of the earlier application as filed. Subject to these conditions, the divisional application will have the same date of filing of the earlier application and will enjoy the right of priority, if this is the case. Moreover, all the Contracting States designated in the earlier application at the time of filing of a European divisional application will be automatically designated in the divisional application.

II. Conditions Required to a European Patent Application

430. According to Article 78 (1) EPC:

(1) A European patent application shall contain:
  (a) a request for the grant of a European patent;
  (b) a description of the invention;
  (c) one or more claims;
  (d) any drawings referred to in the description or the claims;

232. EPC Art. 77.
233. EPC Art. 133.
234. EPC Art. 14(2), Rule 6(1).
235. EPC Art. 76.

(e) an abstract.

and satisfy the requirements laid down in the Implementing Regulations.

431. This is usually called 'regular filing' which includes all constituents of a European patent application.

432. Patent applications shall be subject to the payment of the filing fee and the search fee, which not paid in due time, will give the situation that the application is deemed withdrawn.

433. Under the payment of a designation fee, all the Contracting States are deemed to be designated[236] in the request for grant of a European patent, subject to the condition that the designation of a Contracting State may be withdrawn at any time up to the grant of the European patent.

434. This means that according to Article 79(1) EPC, the applicant shall be deemed to have designated all the Contracting States which are party to the convention at the time the application is filed, but applicants continue to have the option of withdrawing designations pursuant to the provisions of Article 79(3) EPC and may do so at the outset, upon filing the European patent application, if they so wish.

435. Even if the regular filing conditions are not fulfilled, EPC provides the granting of a date of filing of a European patent application[237] if for a set of minimum requirements for according a date of filing, according to a check carried out by the Receiving Section. Subsequent conditions for these minimum requirements have been regulated in full compliance with the PLT (*see* Chapter 2 §2 II).

436. These requirements are satisfied where the documents filed contain:

(a) an indication that a European patent is sought; should be obvious that use of the prescribed request for grant form or the software provided by the EPO for electronic filing, best provides 'the indication that a patent is sought';
(b) information identifying the applicant or allowing the applicant to be contacted; if there are multiple applicants, for the purposes of establishing a filing date, the above information only has to be supplied concerning one of them. Any kind of information which allows the applicant to be contacted will be considered to fulfil this requirement, in particular, the name and address of the applicant's representative. a fax number or a PO box number.
and
(c) a description or reference to a single previous application.

236. EPC Art. 79.
237. EPC Art. 80 and Rule 40.

Where the description is filed by reference to a previously filed application, the reference must contain the following information[238] in order for the application to qualify for a filing date:

(i) the filing date of the previous application;
(ii) its file number;
(iii) the office where it was filed;
(iv) an indication that this reference replaces the description and any drawings.

437. As it can be easily noticed, no reference is made to claims, meaning that it is not necessary that the applicant provide any claims in order to obtain a date of filing. If the application is filed without claims but satisfies all requirements for obtaining a date of filing, the applicant will be requested to provide at least one claim later.[239]

438. Any European patent application must designate the inventor[240] and if the applicant is not the inventor or is not the sole inventor, the designation shall contain a statement indicating the origin of the right to the European patent.

439. Designation is mandatory because, as mentioned, a European patent application must contain a request for the grant of a European patent, the request containing among others, the designation of the inventor. If the designation of the inventor is not made, the EPO must inform the applicant[241] that the application will be refused unless the designation is made within sixteen months of the date of filing of the application, or, if priority is claimed, of the date of priority.

440. However, it is to be mentioned that the inventor designated by the applicant may address to the EPO[242] a written waiver of his right to be mentioned as inventor in the published European patent application and the European patent specification

441. EPC provides a series of substantive conditions on specification which are, in principle, harmonized to all systems of patent law and will be mentioned without detailed commentaries.

442. Thus, the European patent application must:

– respect the principle of unity of invention which means that an application relates to one invention only or to a group of inventions so linked as to form a single general inventive concept;[243]

238. EPC Rule 40(2).
239. EPC Rules 57(c) and 58.
240. EPC Art. 81.
241. EPC Rule 60(1).
242. EPC Rule 20(1).
243. EPC Art. 82.

- disclose the invention in a sufficiently clear and complete manner for it to be carried out by a person skilled in the art;[244]
- contain one or more claims which shall define the matter for which protection is sought, be clear and concise and be supported by the description;[245]
- contain an abstract serving solely for informational purposes and correspondingly it may not be taken into account for interpreting the scope of the protection sought.[246]

443. The link between the inventions required by the principle of 'unity of invention' is, in principle, given[247] by a technical relationship which finds expression in the claims in terms of the same or corresponding special technical features. The 'special technical features' means, in any one claim, the particular technical feature or features that define a contribution that the claimed invention considered as a whole makes over the prior art. Once identified, these special technical features of each invention should be investigated if there is a technical relationship between the inventions and furthermore, whether or not this relationship involves these special technical features, the required relationship being possible even between corresponding technical features.

444. A plurality of independent claims in different categories may constitute a group of inventions so linked as to form a single general inventive concept and usually is permitted[248] one of the following combinations of claims of different categories in the same application:

(i) in addition to an independent claim for a given product, an independent claim for a process specially adapted for the manufacture of the said product, and an independent claim for a use of the said product;
(ii) in addition to an independent claim for a given process, an independent claim for an apparatus or means specifically designed for carrying out the said process; or
(iii) in addition to an independent claim for a given product, an independent claim for a process specially adapted for the manufacture of the said product and an independent claim for an apparatus or means specifically designed for carrying out the said process.

445. The requirement of unity has to be met by the subject matter of the independent claims in the same category and consequently, the implicit or explicit presence in each of the independent claims of special technical features relating to the single general inventive concept is necessary.

244. EPC Art. 83.
245. EPC Art. 84.
246. EPC Art. 85.
247. EPO Guidelines for Examination F–V, 2; November 2017 version.
248. EPO Guidelines for Examination F–V, 2; November 2017 version.

446. The condition for sufficiency of disclosure of the patent application is a formal condition for patentability and therefore needs specific attention. Normally, this condition is met[249] when a detailed description of at least one way of carrying out the invention is given; this meaning that the description must disclose the essential features for carrying out the invention in sufficient detail to render it apparent to the skilled person how to put the invention into practice, without being necessary to be given details of well known ancillary features.

447. Objection for lack of sufficient disclosure should be raised[250] when there are serious doubts, substantiated by verifiable facts.

448. Although the general rule on the burden of proof in the question of sufficiency of disclosure lies with the party raising the objection,[251] where the application as filed does not prove that the claimed invention can be carried out and there are serious doubts as regards the possibility of performing the invention and repeating it as described, the burden of proof regarding this possibility or at least a demonstration of credible success rests with the applicant or the proprietor of the patent.

449. The condition stating that claims must be supported by the description means that an indication for the subject matter of every claim could be found in the description and that the scope of the claims must not be broader than that given by the extent of the description and drawings, and also the contribution to the art.[252]

450. In the same line, Articles 87 to 89 EPC regulate the twelve months priority right, including its claiming and effect, in full line with the international approach (Paris Convention. TRIPS, PCT, PLT).

451. Under EPC, the priority right is recognized for an application for a patent, a utility model, or a utility certificate and probably, two provisions arise from the specific nature and character of this European convention, namely:

- multiple priorities may be claimed in respect of a European patent application, notwithstanding the fact that they originated in different countries;
- if the first filing has been made with an industrial property authority which is not subject to the Paris Convention for the Protection of Industrial Property or the Agreement Establishing the WTO, the full mechanism of priority recognition apply if that authority, according to a communication issued by the President of the EPO, recognizes that a first filing made with the EPO gives rise to a right of priority under conditions and with effects equivalent to those laid down in the Paris Convention.

249. EPO Guidelines for Examination F–III, 51; November 2017 version.
250. T 409/91 and T 694/92.
251. EPO Guidelines for Examination F–III,4; November 2017 version.
252. T 409/91.

452. Article 87(5), as revised by EPC 2000, enables the President of the EPO, rather than the AC, to issue the communication and refers to industrial property authorities rather than to states. These two changes remove[253] this essentially technical issue of recognition of priority rights from the political arena and allow it to be dealt more appropriately and effectively at a technical, working level.

453. In addition, since the terms for recognizing a priority right are well laid down in the Paris Convention, there is no need to set up a comprehensive framework regarding such recognition and a communication noting the de facto mutual recognition of priority rights in conformity with the Paris Convention should suffice. Therefore, the requirement that a bilateral or multilateral agreement be concluded is removed.

454. It could, therefore, be concluded that a valid claim to priority should meet the following conditions:[254]

(i) the previous application was filed in or for a state or WTO member recognized as giving rise to a priority right in accordance with the provisions of the EPC;
(ii) the applicant for the European patent was the applicant, or is the successor in title to the applicant, who made the previous application;
(iii) the European application is made during a period of twelve months from the date of filing of the previous application:
  - the European application is in respect of the same invention as the invention disclosed in the previous application, which must be the 'first application'.

455. The concept of 'the same invention' means that the subject matter of a claim in a European application can be derived by a skilled person directly and unambiguously, using common general knowledge, from the previous application as a whole, meaning that the specific combination of features present in the claim must at least implicitly be disclosed in the previous application.

456. The recognition of a priority right based and claimed on the deposit of an industrial design was consequently rejected.[255]

457. In implementation of Article 87(1) EPC which refers to filings 'in or for' any state party to the Paris Convention or member of the WTO, priority may be claimed of an earlier first filed national application, a previous European application, a previous application filed under another regional patent treaty, or an international application filed under the PCT, including[256] the US 'provisional application for patent'.

253. EPO CA/PL 25/00 Rev. 1; Basic Proposal for the Revision of the European Patent Convention; Munich, 28.07.2000.
254. EPO Guidelines for Examination F–VI,1.3; November 2017 version.
255. J 15/80.
256. EPO -Notice from the President of the EPO dated 26 Jan. 1996, OJ EPO 1996, 81.

458. Where multiple priorities are claimed, time limits are calculated from the earliest date of priority and consequently, the European application must be made within twelve months from the earliest priority date.

459. The priority claim may also be withdrawn[257] and if this is done before the technical preparations for publication of the application are completed, the publication will be deferred until eighteen months after the date of filing of the European application or, where multiple priorities are claimed, the earliest priority date remaining.

460. Based on the fact that the average time of the granting procedure at the EPO (as in most of the Patent Offices) exceeds two years, EPC provides that the payment of renewal fees for the European patent application[258] which are due to the EPO in respect of the third year and each subsequent year, calculated from the date of filing of the application. Obligation of payment for renewal fees terminates with the payment due in respect of the year in which the mention of the grant of the European patent is published in the European Patent Bulletin.

461. If a due renewal fee is not paid in due time, the application is deemed to be withdrawn.

III. Basic Steps in European Patent Grant Procedure

462. Before having a closer look into the EPC provisions on the European patent grant procedure, just to underline that it is a substantive examination procedure, beginning with a formalities examination and a mandatory search and which follows some basic steps, as follows:[259]

257. EPO Guidelines for Examination Part E VIII.8.2; November 2017.
258. EPC Art. 86.
259. Heli Pihlajamaa EPO The European Patent Office and the Patent Granting Procedure; 10.12.2009.

The grant procedure at a glance

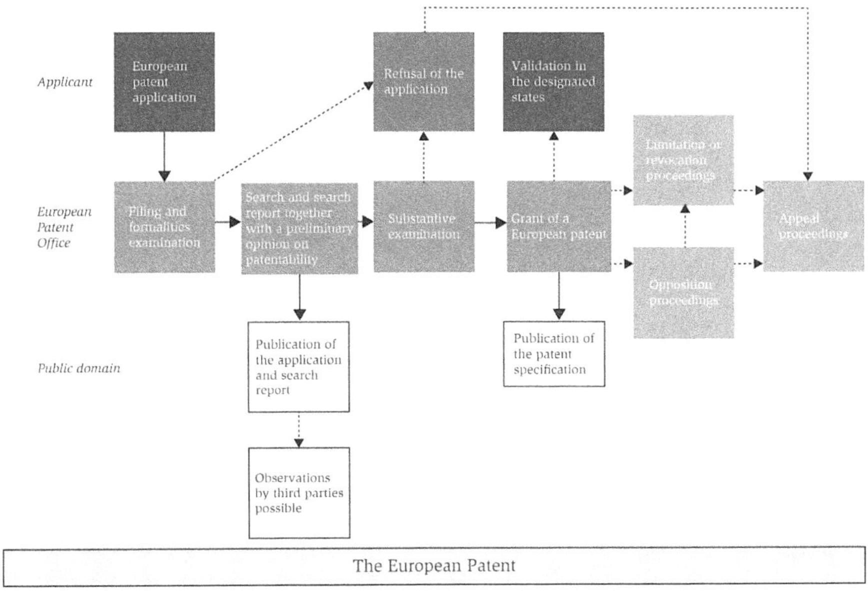

463. The first stage of the procedure comprises of an examination on filing, formalities examination, preparation of the European search report and a preliminary opinion on patentability, and publication of the application and the search report. Responsibility for this stage rests with the Receiving Section and a Search Division.

464. The application is published as soon as possible after the expiry of a period of eighteen months from the date of filing or, where priority is claimed, from the earliest priority date. Upon request from the applicant, the application may, however, be published before that date, provided that there are no formal deficiencies in the application document and the fees have been validly paid. The application is not however published if it has been finally refused or deemed withdrawn or withdrawn before the termination of the technical preparations for publication. The publication contains the description, the claims, and any drawings as filed, including any late-filed missing parts of the description, or drawings, provided that these were not subsequently withdrawn, and specify, where possible, the person(s) designated as the inventor(s).

465. The publication includes usually the European search report but if not published with the application, it will be published separately, including in electronic form. The Receiving Section communicates to the applicant the date on which the

European Patent Bulletin mentions the publication of the European search report and draws his attention to the legal provisions with regard to the request for examination.

466. At the applicant's request, this is followed by the second stage, substantive examination.

467. After the patent has been granted, there may be a further procedure in the form of opposition proceedings or, upon request of the patentee, limitation or revocation proceedings.

468. The second stage comprises substantive examination which could lead to a decision to grant a European patent or refusal of the patent application. Substantive examination is made at the applicant's request who, in principle, should base his decision after a due consideration of the conclusions drafted in the European search report and a preliminary opinion on patentability.

469. After the grant of the patent, there may be opposition proceedings involving third parties as opponents. Responsibility for examining oppositions rests within the Opposition Divisions which are composed in the same way as the Examining Divisions, except that only one member of the Opposition Division may have been involved in the earlier grant proceedings, and that member is not allowed to chair the division.

470. After the grant of the patent, the patent proprietor himself may initiate revocation or limitation proceedings.

471. Appeal proceedings constitute a special procedure regarding the appeals which may be filed against decisions taken by the Receiving Section, the Examining Divisions, the Opposition Divisions or the Legal Division. A decision which does not terminate proceedings as regards one of the parties can only be appealed together with the final decision unless the decision allows separate appeal.

472. Decisions on appeals are taken by the Boards of Appeal.

473. In certain cases, it may be possible to file a petition for review by the Enlarged Board of Appeal.

A. *Examination under Receiving Section and a Search Division*

474. Examination starts naturally on filing and, as to formal requirements,[260] whether the application satisfies the requirements for the accordance of a date of filing and if the mentioned minimal conditions are not fulfilled, the application is not dealt with as a European patent application.

260. EPC Art. 90.

475. Contrarily, if the European patent application has been accorded a date of filing, the EPO examines whether the requirements of having a regular filing have been satisfied.

476. If it is found that there are deficiencies which may be corrected, EPC provides the possibility for the applicant an opportunity to correct them. If any deficiency noted in the examination process is not corrected, the European patent application will be refused unless a different legal consequence is provided for by the EPC. Where the deficiency concerns the right of priority, there is no reason to refuse the application, but the application will not take the benefit of the right of priority.

477. If examination as to formalities ends successfully, the EPO draws up and publishes[261] a European search report in respect of the European patent application on the basis of the claims with due regard to the description and any drawings.

478. The drafted search report has a particular importance in the granting procedure, because on one side it establishes the state of the art by mentioning the documents and their degree of relevance for the assessment of patentability, and on the other side, its publication enables both applicants and third parties to express an eventual position on the continuation of the patenting procedure. The EPC provides for the possibility offered to the applicant to request continuation of the examination only after the search report has become available.[262]

479. The application is published as soon as possible after the expiry of a period of eighteen months from the date of filing or, where priority is claimed, from the earliest priority date. Upon request from the applicant, the application may, however, be published before that date, provided that there are no formal deficiencies in the application document and the fees have been validly paid.

480. The applicant may withdraw his application[263] at any time as long as the application is pending, provided that no third party has proven to the EPO that he has initiated proceedings concerning entitlement to the application.

481. The application is not however published if it has been finally refused or deemed withdrawn or withdrawn before the termination of the technical preparations for publication. The publication contains the description, the claims and any drawings as filed, including any late-filed missing parts of the description, or drawings, provided that these were not subsequently withdrawn, and specify, where possible, the person(s) designated as the inventor(s).

482. The publication includes usually the European search report but if not published with the application, it will be published separately, including in electronic

261. EPC Art. 91 and 92.
262. EPC Rule 70(1).
263. EPO Guidelines for Examination Part E VIII.8.1; November 2017.

form. The Receiving Section communicates to the applicant the date on which the European Patent Bulletin mentions the publication of the European search report and draws his attention to the legal provisions with regard to the request for examination.

483. The applicant is required to respond to the search opinion within a prescribed time limit and if the applicant fails to respond to the search opinion on time, the application is deemed to be withdrawn.[264]

484. The European patent application is published at the same time as the specification of the European patent when the decision to grant the patent becomes effective before the expiry of the period of eighteen months from the date of filing or, if priority has been claimed, from the date of priority.

B. Substantive Examination

485. As mentioned, examination of the European patent application[265] is performed at the request of the applicant by an EPO examination division which, subject to the condition that the examination fee has been paid, analyses whether the application and the invention to which it relates meet the requirements of the EPC.

486. The applicant may request examination of the European patent application[266] up to six months after the date on which the European Patent Bulletin mentions the publication of the European search report. The request may not be withdrawn.

487. If no request for examination has been made in due time, the application is deemed to be withdrawn.

488. If the examination reveals that the application or the invention to which it relates does not meet the requirements of the EPC, the applicant is invited, as often as necessary, to file his observations and where the case might be, to amend the application.

489. If the applicant fails to reply in due time to any communication from the Examining Division, the application is deemed to be withdrawn

490. Examining Divisions are made up of three technically qualified examiners who may, if necessary, be joined by a legally qualified examiner. Until a decision has to be taken on the application, its examination is, as a rule, entrusted to one of the technically qualified examiners who are responsible for issuing the requisite communications and for discussing the application with the applicant.

---

264. EPC Rule 70a(3).
265. EPC Art. 94.
266. EPC Regulation Rule 70(1).

491. If oral proceedings are requested by the applicant or arranged at the office's initiative, they are held before the full Examining Division. The final decision on the grant of the patent or refusal of the application is also a matter for the full Examining Division.

492. The Examining Division takes a decision[267] to grant a European patent if the European patent application and the invention to which it relates meet the requirements of the EPC, or contrarily, to refuse the application if it is of the opinion that the European patent application or the invention to which it relates does not meet the requirements of the EEPC, unless EPC provides for a different legal consequence.

493. The decision to grant a European patent becomes effective on the date on which the mention of the grant is published in the European Patent Bulletin.

494. The final decision on the grant of the patent or refusal of the application is also a matter for the full Examining Division.

495. A decision to refuse the application cannot be issued[268] without first a communication for examination having been sent or oral proceedings having been held. Therefore, the Examining Division may not refuse the application directly after the reply to the search opinion or directly after the reply to the WO-ISA under Rule 161(1), even if the objections raised in the search opinion or WO-ISA remain the same and there is no pending request for oral proceedings.

496. The refusal can be issued if, despite the applicant's submissions, objections persist after the applicant's reply.

497. The publication of the specification of the European patent, containing the description, claims (in the three official languages) and any drawings[269] take place as soon as possible after the mention of the grant of the European patent has been published in the European Patent Bulletin.

498. It is to be noted that the current wording of Article 98 EPC – after the revision brought by EPC 2000 contains the phrase 'as soon as possible' which is meant to make clear that for different reasons it is not always technically possible to publish the specification on the same day as the mention of the grant.

499. The front page of the published specification shows *inter alia* the Contracting States which are still designated at the time of grant (or the designation of which has been withdrawn after completion of the technical preparations for printing).

---

267. EPC Art. 97.
268. EPO Guidelines for Examination Part C V. 14; November 2017.
269. EPC Art. 98.

500. The specification of the European patent is not published if the application is withdrawn before termination of the technical preparations for publication.[270]

501. As soon as the European patent specification has been published, the EPO issues the proprietor with a certificate attesting that the European patent has been granted to the person named in the certificate and where there is more than one proprietor, each of them is issued with a certificate.[271]

C. Accelerated Prosecution Procedure of European Applications

502. Applicants may require a faster search or examination procedure by asking their applications be processed under the programme for accelerated prosecution of EP applications (PACE).[272]

503. A PACE request may be filed only once during each stage of the procedure, that is, search and examination, and for one application at a time. A PACE request filed during the search will not trigger accelerated examination. If the applicant wishes to have the application examined in an accelerated manner, a PACE request may be filed once the application has entered the examination phase.

504. An application will be taken out of the PACE programme if:

- the PACE request has been withdrawn;
- the applicant has requested an extension of time limits;
- the application has been refused, withdrawn, or deemed to be withdrawn.

505. For an accelerated search, the EPO strives to issue the extended/partial European search report within six months from the filing date or from the priority date.

506. For European patent applications which do claim priority (second filings), the EPO makes every effort, on receipt of a PACE request, to issue the extended/partial European search report within six months from receipt of the request.

507. An accelerated search can only start:

(i) after receipt of the applicant's response to a communication, or expiry of the respective time limit;
(ii) in all cases when the application documents on the filing are complete enough for the extended search report to be drawn up;

270. EPC Rule 73.
271. EPC Rule 74.
272. EPO Guidelines for Examination E VII 4.2; November 2017 edition.

(iii) for PCT applications entering the European phase where the EPO did not act as (S)ISA after expiry of the six-month period, even if acceleration has been requested under the PACE programme;

508. Accelerated examination can, in principle, be requested at any time after the Examining Division has assumed responsibility for the application.

509. When accelerated examination is requested, the EPO makes every effort to issue the next office action within three months of receipt by the Examining Division of the application, the applicant's response or the request for accelerated examination (whichever is later).

510. The EPO strives to produce subsequent examination communications within three months of receipt of the applicant's reply, provided that the application is still being processed under the PACE programme.

§6. Opposition Procedure and Limitation and Revocation Procedures

I. Legal Nature

511. Opposition is a post-grant procedure provided for in the EPC which allows third parties the opportunity to bring about *ex tunc* revocation or limitation of a European patent and thus challenging the grant of patent considered to have been performed on false grounds. It thus differs from the more encountered procedure in other patent systems, where the grant of the patent is prevented of refused within a pre-grant opposition.

512. In fact, the opposition at the EPO is the only opportunity in which to challenge a granted European patent as a single title before it becomes a bundle of national patents and since opposing only involves proceedings before EPO as a single office, it is much simpler than managing multiple actions for revocation across several jurisdictions based on its own national law and consequently, it is a very cost-effective procedure.

513. It is a uniform and centralized procedure because it applies to the European patent in all the Contracting States in which that patent has effect.

514. There are some important reasons for opposing a patent, among them, being:[273]

- Infringement – where is considered that granted patent might unfairly infringe a valid prior patent;

273. Closa Daniel, Beaucé Gaëtan The Opposition Procedure and Limitation and Revocation Procedures; EPO 26–30/11/2012.

- Licensing/cross-licensing – if a granted patent might lead to a necessary licensing agreement considered by the opponent as unjustified;
- Strategy – necessity of eliminating the technological barrier put by a granted patent to own researches developed by opponent;
- Patent intelligence – patent has been granted based on a prior developed technology kept as secret;
- Political/ethical reasons – considered usually, patents that have been granted for invention(s) excluded/excepted from patentability, for political/ethical reasons.

515. The principle of party disposition *ne ultra petita* applies to the EPO opposition procedure.[274]

516. Thus, the opposition proceedings allow,[275] during a limited period of time, a centralized action for revocation of a European patent brought before and decided by the EPO, and constitute an exception to the general rule under the EPC that the granted European patent is no longer within the competence of the EPO but becomes a bundle of patents within the jurisdiction of the designated Contracting States.

517. This procedure takes place[276] at a moment when the proprietor benefits in each designated Contracting State of the same rights as would be conferred by a national patent granted in that state.

518. Opposition is an *interpartes* procedure between opponent(s) and the proprietor of the patent who should be treated equally. EPC provides that in the situation where a person provides evidence that, following a final decision, he has been entered in the patent register of a Contracting State instead of the previous proprietor, such a person shall, at his request, replace the previous proprietor in respect of such state. The previous proprietor and the person making the request will be regarded as joint proprietors if both so request.

519. The opposition procedure is a purely administrative procedure and it is not provided as an extension of the examination procedure[277] The grounds for opposition as already presented, are essentially the same as the grounds for revocation under national law (*see* Chapter 3 §9 II).

520. As an administrative act, the opposition procedure has[278] neither suspensive effect nor the effect of transferring the case to a superior instance and differs in substance from the appeal procedure, which – as will be presented further – must be regarded as a judicial one.

274. Dybdahl Lise – European Patents; pg. 183; Carls Heymans Verlag KG 2001.
275. EPO Case Law of the Boards of Appeal IV D1; 8th Edition July 2016.
276. G 9/91 OJ 1993.
277. G 1/84, OJ 1985.
278. T 695/89, OJ 1993.

II. Grounds of Opposition

521. EPC provides three main grounds for opposition,[279] namely:

- the subject matter of the European patent is not patentable, that is, questioned novelty and/or inventive step and /or industrially applicability and/or exclusions/ exceptions from patentability;
- the European patent does not disclose the invention in a manner sufficiently clear and complete for it to be carried out by a person skilled in the art;
- the subject matter of the European patent extends beyond the content of the application as filed, or if the patent was granted on a divisional application or on a new application, beyond the content of the earlier application as filed.

522. If it is not too much to add the first and last ground considering either patentability considerations exposed already within Chapter 3 §5 II or non-allowable amendments beyond the original application as filed, the second ground refers to the situation where the patent does not provide sufficient information to allow someone skilled in the relevant field of technology to perform the invention in a repeatable and controllable manner.

III. Procedural Steps

A. Entitlement to File and Opposition

523. The EPC case law held that EPC does not require that the opponent have his own interest in the outcome of the opposition proceedings and accordingly [280] the motives of the opponent were, in principle, irrelevant because the law left to 'any person' the opportunity to file an opposition and not to as 'any person interested', which would contravene to that conclusion.

524. Anyway, only an existing natural or legal person may be a party to opposition proceedings.[281]

525. The purpose and special nature of the opposition procedure indicates that the patent proprietors may not oppose their own patent and accordingly patent proprietors were not covered by the expression 'any person', the legal provisions being clearly based on the assumption that the opponent is a person other than the patent proprietor and that the opposition proceedings are always inter partes.[282]

279. EPC Art.100.
280. G 1/84 OJ 1985.
281. T 353/95.
282. G 9/93 OJ 1994.

526. As will be detailed later on, in order to solve a possible requested intervention in this respect from the part of the patent proprietor, a procedure has been provided starting with EPC 2000 for limitation or revocation of a European patent at the request of the patent proprietor.

527. The EPO case law clarified the possibility to fill for opposition on behalf of a third party[283] acting for some other person by considering that filing the opposition formally renders this person the legitimate opponent and therefore the fact that the opponent is acting on behalf of a third party does not render the opposition inadmissible

B. Procedure and Decisions

528. According to opposition procedure, within nine months of the publication of the mention of the grant of the questioned European patent in the European Patent Bulletin, any person may give notice to the EPO of opposition[284] to that patent. Opposition is considered to have been filed subject to the payment of an opposition fee.

529. Examination of the opposition[285] follows some procedural steps which consist, in the formalities stage, allocation to an Opposition Division, examination and communications, and eventual publication of a new specification of the European patent.

530. According to Article 114(1), the EPO examines facts on its own motion and is not restricted to those put forward by the parties.[286] The Opposition Divisions, as well as Boards of Appeal, may decide on the revocation or maintenance of the questioned patent only to the extent to which the patent is opposed in the notice of opposition and consequently opposition proceedings cover[287] strictly the specific parts of the European patent for which the grounds of opposition have been related.

531. If the opposition is found as admissible, the allocated Opposition Division examines whether at least one of the three mentioned grounds for opposition prejudices the maintenance of the European patent, and may decide to:

- revoke the patent, if at least one ground for opposition prejudices the maintenance of the European patent or if the amendments made by the proprietor of the European patent during the opposition proceedings, the patent and the invention to which it relates are found to not meet the requirements of the EPC;
- reject the opposition; if no grounds for oppositions are found;

283. G 3/97 OJ 1999.
284. EPC Art. 99.
285. EPC Art.101.
286. Dybdahl Lise – European Patents; pg. 183; Carls Heymans Verlag KG 2001.
287. G 9/91. OJ 1993.

– maintain the patent as amended if the amendments made by the proprietor of the European patent during the opposition proceedings, the patent and the invention to which it relates are found to meet the requirements of the EPC.

532. During the examination procedure, parties are invited by the relevant division to file as often as necessary, observations on communications from another party or issued by itself.

533. If the European patent is maintained as amended, a new specification of the European patent is published by the EPO [288] as soon as possible after the mention of the decision to oppose has been published in the European Patent Bulletin.

534. As mentioned, the limitation or revocation will take effect ex tunc.[289]

535. EPC gives the opportunity to an assumed infringer to intervene in opposition proceedings[290] after the opposition period has expired if it proves that proceedings for infringement of the same patent have been instituted against him or, following a request of the proprietor of the patent to cease alleged infringement, the assumed infringer has instituted proceedings for a ruling that he is not infringing the patent.

536. If no opposition is filed within nine months of publication of the mention of grant, the patent proprietor is informed and an appropriate entry is published in the European Patent Bulletin.[291]

537. If this is the case, an admissible intervention shall be treated as an opposition.

538. EPC 2000 introduced the new Article 105a-c which provides a central administrative procedure open to the proprietor at any time after the grant of the patent meant to solve the problem of 'self-opposition' which, under previous approach, was negatively concluded by the well known decision[292] that 'a European patent cannot be opposed by its own proprietor.'

539. Under this extended limitation procedure, the European patent may be limited or revoked *ab initio* (*see* Article 68 EPC) at the request of the patent proprietor. Limitation or revocation may be requested at any time although, precedence must always be given to opposition proceedings. Making the limitation procedure ex parte and doing away with an examination of the patentability of the residual patent guarantees a speedy decision from the EPO.

288. EPC Art. 103.
289. EPC Art. 68.
290. EPC Art. 105.
291. EPC Art. 129(a).
292. G 0009/93 (Opposition by Patent Proprietor).

540. Under Article 105a(1), a European patent may be revoked or limited, by an amendment of the claims, at the request of the proprietor subject to payment of a fee and the fulfilment of the criteria for admissibility (written request, joint filing by multiple proprietors, documentation to be filed with request, etc.) as set out in the Implementing Regulations.

541. Article 105a (2) EPC clarifies the relation[293] between the limitation and opposition proceedings. The priority it gives to opposition proceedings prevents limitation procedures occurring where opposition has already been lodged. The procedure is to be followed in the rare situations where opposition proceedings are initiated following the valid lodging of a request for limitation or revocation. In that respect, the intention is that, if revocation is requested, limitation proceedings are to continue and the patent is to be revoked or not as appropriate. If amendment of the patent is requested, limitation proceedings are to be stayed until opposition proceedings have been completed.

542. Being initiated by the proprietor of the European patent itself, the procedure in this particular case is ex parte and normally would lead to a rapid processing by the EPO, in maximum. two months. This is due to the fact that it must include amended claims that are limited in scope but patentability conditions of the resulting patent are not examined.

543. The procedural steps exposed for normal opposition, including publication of the amended specification of the European patent, are valid *mutatis mutandis.*

544. The request for revocation or limitation may be filed at any time after the grant of the patent but not while opposition proceedings in respect of the European patent are pending. Decisions on the revocation or limitation of European patents are taken by the Examining Divisions.

545. In terms of statistics, in 2016,[294] the EPO issued some 4,100 opposition decisions, with an opposition rate of 4%. In these cases, 72% of the patents were upheld either as granted (32%) or in an amended form (40%), and these figures are indicating the EPO as a successful 'patent granting machine'.

C. Accelerated Processing of Oppositions

546. EPC provides an accelerated processing of oppositions which may be requested by a party to the opposition proceedings in cases where an infringement action in respect of a European patent is pending before a national court of a Contracting State. The request may be filed at any time, in written reasoned form. The

293. EPO CA/PL 25/00 Rev. 1; Basic Proposal for the Revision of the European Patent Convention; Munich.
294. EPO Annual Report 2016 - Searches, Examinations, Oppositions; pg. 1–3.

EPO may also accelerate the processing of the opposition if[295] it is informed by the national court or competent authority of a Contracting State that infringement actions are pending

§7. APPEALS PROCEDURE

I. Legal Nature

547. The appeals procedure within the EPO are the attribute of the various Boards of Appeal which consist of:

- the Enlarged Board of Appeal;
- the Technical Boards of Appeal;
- the Legal Board of Appeal; and
- the Disciplinary Board of Appeal.

548. The Boards of Appeal are[296] the first and final judicial instance in the procedures before the EPO, being independent of the office in their decision.

549. According to several decisions of the Enlarged Board,[297] the appeal procedure is to be considered as a judicial procedure proper to an administrative court rather than a purely administrative procedure and[298] is generally recognized that the board members' function as judges.

550. Appeal proceedings are wholly separate and independent from the proceedings at first instance. Their function is[299] to give a judicial decision upon the correctness of a separate earlier decision taken by a department.

551. The Boards of Appeal may be seen as having the status of judicial authorities since they embody all the features of such an authority in their decisions. The members of the boards are not bound by any instructions and are obliged to comply only with the provisions of the EPC.[300]

552. This chapter should be read in conjunction with the Rules of Procedure of the Boards of Appeal of the EPO [301]

295. EPO Guidelines for Examination Part E VIII.5; November 2017.
296. G 3/08 OJ 2011.
297. G 1/99 OJ 2001; G 9/91, OJ 1993; G 8/91 OJ 1993.
298. G 2301/15.
299. T 34/90, OJ 1992; G 9/91, OJ 1993.
300. G 1/97 OJ 2000.
301. Decision of the Administrative Council of 25 October 2007 approving amendments to the Rules of Procedure of the Boards of Appeal of the European Patent Office, OJ EPO 2007, 536.

II. Procedural Steps

553. Decisions subject to appeal[302] could originate from the Receiving Section, Examining Divisions, Opposition Divisions, and the Legal Division and once the appeal procedure starts, it has a suspensive effect.

554. Under Article 106(1) EPC, an appeal has suspensive effect, meaning that[303] the contested decision had no legal effect until the appeal is resolved otherwise, the appeal would be nugatory. It also means[304] that the consequences following an appealed decision do not immediately occur after the decision has been taken.

555. The decisions which do not terminate proceedings, as regards, one of the parties can only be appealed together with the final decision unless a separate appeal is provided in the decision.

556. Persons entitled to appeal and to be parties to appeal proceedings[305] are primarily any party to proceedings adversely affected by a decision but also any other parties to the proceedings, by right.

557. Notice of appeal shall be filed[306] at the EPO within two months of notification of the decision and a statement must be filed within four months of notification of the decision, setting out the grounds of appeal.

558. EPC provides the possibility of an interlocutory revision[307] by giving to the department whose decision is contested to rectify its decision if it considers the appeal to be admissible and well founded, except where the appellant is opposed by another party to the proceedings.

559. The finding that an appeal is admissible may be given in an interlocutory decision and EPC provides that the boards have to examine whether an appeal is admissible before considering its merits. An interlocutory decision is usually taken[308] where the points of law concerning admissibility are of general significance and require a speedy decision.

560. If the appeal is not allowed within three months of receipt of the statement of grounds, it is remitted to the Board of Appeal without delay, and without comment.

302. EPC Art. 106.
303. J 28/94 OJ 1995.
304. J 28/03 OJ 2005.
305. EPC Art. 107.
306. EPC Art. 108.
307. EPC Art. 109.
308. T 152/82, OJ 1984.

561. If the appeal is admissible,[309] the Board of Appeal examines its ability.to allow decisions in respect of appeals.[310]

562. The admissibility of an appeal can only be assessed as a whole because it is considered that there is no support in the EPC for a notion of 'partial admissibility' of an appeal[311]

563. R. 100(1) EPC stipulates that, unless otherwise provided, the provisions relating to proceedings before the department which had taken the decision impugned shall apply to appeal proceedings.

564. Once the allowability of the appeal has been checked, the decisions of the Board of Appeal [312] may be either to exercise any power within the competence of the department which was responsible for the decision appealed or remit the case to that department for further prosecution In this last situation, that department shall be bound by the *ratio decidendi* of the Board of Appeal in so far as the facts are the same. If the decision under appeal was taken by the Receiving Section, the Examining Division shall also be bound by the *ratio decidendi* of the Board of Appeal.

565. It is possible to have an accelerated processing[313] asked by parties with a legitimate interest. The boards can speed up an appeal as far as the procedural regulations allow. Requests for accelerated processing must be submitted to the competent board either at the beginning of or during proceedings and must include reasons for the urgency together with relevant documents.

III. Decisions or Opinions of the Enlarged Board of Appeal

566. Decisions or opinions of the Enlarged Board of Appeal[314] are requested in order to ensure uniform application of the law or must be solved by a point of law of fundamental importance.

567. Non-uniform application of the law under the previous point refers to the non-uniform application of the law by the Boards of Appeal.

568. Contrary to that situation, a lack of uniformity between the law as applied by the Boards of Appeal and national courts can, in theory, bring to the fore a point of law of fundamental importance.[315]

569. Decisions may be requested by:

---

309. EPC Art. 110.
310. EPC Art. 111.
311. EPO-Case Law of the Boards of Appeal IV E2; 8th Edition July 2016.
312. EPC Art. 112.
313. EPO Guidelines for Examination Part E VIII.6; November 2017.
314. EPC Art. 113.
315. T 712/10.

(i) A Board of Appeal, which, during proceedings on a case and either of its own motion or following a request from a party to the appeal, considers that a decision is required for the above purposes. The parties to the appeal proceedings shall be parties to the proceedings before the Enlarged Board of Appeal. The decision of the Enlarged Board of Appeal shall be binding on the Board of Appeal in respect of the appeal in question.
(ii) The President of the EPO, where two Boards of Appeal have given different decisions on identical or similar question(s).

570. Where a board considers necessary to deviate from an earlier opinion or decision of the Enlarged Board, the question must be referred to the Enlarged Board.

571. The purpose of the presidential referral right upper mentioned is[316] to establish uniformity of law within the European patent system and having regard to this purpose, the notion 'different decisions' has to be understood restrictively in the sense of 'conflicting decisions'.

572. Parties to appeal proceedings adversely affected by the decision of the Board of Appeal may file a petition for review of the decision by the Enlarged Board of Appeal[317] based exclusively on at least one of the following grounds:

(a) a member of the Board of Appeal took part in the decision where he had any personal interest, or if he has previously been involved as representatives of one of the parties, or if he participated in the decision under appeal, or despite being excluded pursuant to a previous decision;
(b) the Board of Appeal included a person not appointed as a member of the Boards of Appeal;
(c) occurred a fundamental violation of the right to be heard;
(d) any other fundamental procedural defect defined in the Implementing Regulations occurred in the appeal proceedings; or
(e) a criminal act established under the conditions laid down in the Implementing Regulations may have had an impact on the decision.

573. The petition for review has no suspensive effect.

574. If based on paragraph 2(a) to (d) (EPC Article 112a), the petition must be filed within two months of notification of the decision of the Board of Appeal. If based on paragraph 2(e) (EPC Article 112a), the petition must be filed within two months of the date on which the criminal act has been established and in any event no later than five years from notification of the decision of the Board of Appeal.

575. The Enlarged Board of Appeal examines the petition for review and if it is allowable, sets aside the decision and shall re-open proceedings before the Boards of Appeal.

---

316. EPO-Case Law of the Boards of Appeal; IV F 2.4.3; 8th Edition July 2016.
317. EPC Art. 112 a.

576. The continuation of the appeal proceedings must stop once the appeal had been withdrawn.

577. As mentioned, the Enlarged Board consists of five legally and two technically qualified members wherefrom, the Chairman must be legally qualified and the composition being under the condition that if the question is referred to the Enlarged Board by a Board of Appeal, at least four members of the Enlarged Board must not have taken part in the proceedings before the referring board.

578. Any person who, in a designated Contracting State, has in good faith used or made effective and serious preparations for using the invention which is the subject of a published European patent application or a related patent in the period between the decision of the Board of Appeal and publication of the decision of the Enlarged Board of Appeal on the petition may, without payment, continue such use in the course of his business or for the needs thereof.

579. The Boards of Appeal currently receive about 2,500 new cases per year and settle about 2,300 cases.

IV. Governance of the Boards of Appeal

580. In order to strengthen the boards' organizational and managerial autonomy and increase their efficiency, the AC approved at its 148th meeting on 29 and 30 June 2016, a comprehensive reform package concerning the Boards of Appeal.

581. To this end, the Boards of Appeal have been reorganized[318] as a separate unit within the EPO called the Boards of Appeal Unit. The new unit is managed by the President of the Boards of Appeal – a new position – who is hierarchically independent of the President of the Office and solely responsible to the AC. The President of the Boards of Appeal is the administrative head of the boards. He/She is, at the same time, the Chairman of the Enlarged Board of Appeal.

582. The members and Chairmen are appointed for a term of five years. The President of the Boards of Appeal is hierarchically independent of the President of the EPO and responsible only to the AC. In an Act of Delegation, the President of the EPO delegated to the President of the Boards of Appeal powers relating to the appointment and re-appointment of members of the Boards of Appeal and to managerial and disciplinary matters.

583. A new subsidiary body of the AC, the Boards of Appeal Committee, will act as a link between the boards and the AC. Its primary role is to advise the President of the Boards of Appeal on managerial and organizational issues. The committee is also responsible for adopting the Rules of Procedure of the Boards of Appeal and the Enlarged Board of Appeal.

318. EPO-Annual report 2016.

584. In their activities the Boards of Appeal are guided by a set of principles:[319]

- justice and efficiency;
- high-quality standards;
- consistent and predictable procedures;
- consistency in their jurisprudence;
- easy accessibility to the public of their decisions.

§8. COMMON PROVISIONS

I. Common Provisions on Procedure

585. EPC warrants the right of the applicant and of the parties concerned to be heard and decisions[320] are based on grounds or evidence on which they have had the opportunity to present their comments.

586. In this respect, the EPO examines and decides upon the European patent application or the European patent only in the text submitted to it or agreed by the applicant, or the proprietor of the patent

587. In proceedings before it,[321] the EPO examines the facts of its own motion without restricting in this examination to the facts, evidence, and arguments provided by the parties and the relief sought. The EPO is, thus, free to disregard facts or evidence which are not submitted in due time by the parties concerned.

588. Following the publication of the European patent application, third parties may present observations[322] concerning the patentability of the invention to which the application or patent relates. Observations must be restricted to the substantive requirements of the EPC.

589. The EPO case law pointed out[323] that the only requirement relating to the entitlement to submit third-party observations was that the third party would not be a party to the proceedings, without being analysed whether the third party was acting in its own name or on behalf of someone else.

590. If an applicant fails to observe a time limit[324] vis-à-vis the EPO, he may request further processing of the European patent application and the EPO grants

319. EPO- About the Boards of Appeal; https://www.epo.org/law-practice/case-law-appeals/about-the-boards-of-appeal.html.
320. EPC Art. 113.
321. EPC Art.114.
322. EPC Art. 115.
323. T 1224/09.
324. EPC Art. 121.

the request subject to the legal requirements be met and consequently the legal consequences of the failure to observe the time limit are deemed not to have ensued, otherwise, EPO shall reject the request.

591. EPC provides the possibility of re-establishment of rights[325] for an applicant or for a proprietor of a European patent who, in spite of all due care required by the circumstances having been taken, was unable to observe a time limit vis-à-vis the EPO. It may be made upon request if the non-observance of this time limit has the direct consequence of causing the refusal of the European patent application or of a request, or the deeming of the application to have been withdrawn, or the revocation of the European patent, or the loss of any other right or means of redress.

592. The upper provision indicates that the re-establishment of rights may be granted to both the applicant and the proprietor of a European patent, but this remedy in general, are not available to opponents.

593. The EPO case law held,[326] however, that an opponent as appellant might have his rights re-established if he had failed to observe the time limit for filing the statement of grounds of appeal. It has been considered that the general legal principle recognized in the Contracting States of the EPC must be applied[327] so that all parties to proceedings before a court must be accorded the same procedural rights as a principle deriving from the general principle of equality before the law. Under this principle, an opponent must not be treated differently from the patent proprietor as that would result in unjustifiable discrimination against him.

594. If the legal conditions are met, the EPO grants the request and the legal consequences of the failure to observe the time limit shall be deemed not to have ensued, otherwise, EPO shall reject the request.

595. Any person who, in a designated Contracting State has, in good faith, used or made effective and serious preparations for using an invention which is the subject of a published European patent application or a European patent in the period between the loss of rights previously referred and publication of re-establishment of those rights of the mentioned in the European Patent Bulletin may, without payment, continue such use in the course of his business or for the needs thereof.

596. The EPO case law expressed the view that third-party rights of use arose only[328] where the restoration related to an already published European patent application or a European patent and accordingly third-party rights to use the invention where an applicant's rights have been lost and restored cannot arise if the loss and restoration of the applicant's rights occur before publication of the European patent application

325. EPC Art. 122.
326. G 1/86 OJ 1987.
327. EPO-Case Law of the Boards of Appeal; II E 2.1; 8th edition, July 2016.
328. J 5/79 OJ 1980.

597. The European patent application or a European patent may be amended[329] in proceedings before the EPO, the applicant having at least one opportunity to amend the application on his own volition. The said amendments are to be drafted in such a way that on one side, it contains no subject matter which extends beyond the content of the application as filed and on the other side, without extending the protection it confers.

598. EPC provides[330] the possibility for the EPO to invite the applicant to provide 'information on prior art, taken into consideration in national or regional patent proceedings and concerning an invention to which the European patent application relates.' If the applicant fails to reply in due time to the invitation issued by the EPO, the European patent application shall be deemed to be withdrawn

599. Since the priority of a national patent application is claimed for about 90% of European patent applications, the EPO is in fact in a position to request relevant information about corresponding national or regional applications – particularly, first filings on which the priority is based.

600. In particular, the search results for these applications or other data concerning the relevant prior art considered in proceedings before a national or regional office can be helpful to the EPO when processing the corresponding European patent application in order to speed up the European grant procedure and enhance the quality of search and substantive examination.

II. Representation

601. Great complexity of the EPC and of the patenting procedure implementing it at the EPO are relevant factors which lead to the fact that most of the applicants are, in fact, represented by professionals who should have necessary skills to advise them and to manage adequately on their behalf, the European patent applications and patents granted on their bases

602. According to the principles of representation in proceedings before the EPO,[331] as a general rule, there is no obligation to be represented by a professional representative but no person shall be compelled to be represented by him/her.

603. However, representation by a professional representative and acting through him in all proceedings established by the EPC is compulsory for natural or legal persons not having their residence or principal place of business in an EPC Contracting State. Filing a European patent application may be performed by any person.

329. EPC Art. 123.
330. EPC Art. 124.
331. EPC Art. 133–134.

604. Representation of persons who must be represented and persons who need not be represented but want to be represented must be by a professional representative, or, if the party is an EPC Member State, the representation may be by an authorized employee or by a legal practitioner. A legal practitioner representing a party before the EPO must be qualified in an EPC Contracting State must have his place of business in that state and must be entitled in that state to act as a professional representative in patent matters. Both authorized employees and legal practitioners 'must file a signed authorization or a reference to a general authorization already on file'. Within these restrictions, a party may be represented in the chosen by him manner.

605. According to the EPC, EPO manages the list of professional representatives and representation of natural or legal persons in relevant proceedings is restricted only to the names appearing on that list.

606. This list is opened to natural persons who meet the following cumulative conditions:

- are nationals of a Contracting State;
- have a place of business or employment in a Contracting State; and
- have passed the European qualifying examination, organized and managed by the EPO, at very high standards of competence.

607. The objective of the list of professional representatives is to provide a survey of particularly qualified representatives in patent matters.[332]

608. The previous Article 163 EPC 1973 has been integrated into Article 134(3) EPC 2000 in a simplified form as a permanent provision of the EPC and refers to the so-called grandfather clause.

609. Aiming to be a safeguard business for national patent attorneys originating from new accessing states to the EPC, this clause provides that during a period of one year from the date on which the accession of a state to this convention takes effect, entry on that list may also be requested by any natural person who, similar to general case, is a national of a Contracting State and has his place of business or employment in the state having acceded to the convention, but who, instead passing a qualifying examination, can prove by adequate certifications, that they have an entitlement to act before national industrial property office by a special professional qualification, or proving minimum five years of professional experience.

610. In special circumstances and supported by relevant proofs that the applicant has acquired the requisite qualification in another way, the President of the EPO may grant certain exemptions from the above conditions of representation.

332. D 14/93, OJ 1997.

611. All professional representatives acting before the EPO must be members of the EPI established on 21 October 1977, by the AC, which adopted the Regulation on the establishment of an institute of professional representatives before the EPO. The EPI is governed by a council which is elected by the members of the respective national constituencies and by a board elected by the council, which includes its President. The EPI Council has adopted internal regulations governing its conduct and functioning.

612. A relevant decision of the AC[333] made important changes in the governance of the EPI according to which following each election of the council, the latter elected a board from among its members.

613. The council has the management and control of the affairs of the Institute and the right to delegate powers. The council equally has the power to make regulations governing the conduct of the business of the Institute and its constituent and any subsidiary bodies.

614. The distribution of powers is exercised between the President which represents the Institute and the board which exercises powers delegated to it by the council.

615. A number of committees, including numerous subcommittees and working groups, are managing the large volume of tasks and assignments faced by the EPI.

616. The AC has a large competence[334] to adopt and amend provisions governing all aspects connected with the activity of the EPI, including EPOrg; the qualifications and training required of a person for admission to the European qualifying examination and the conduct of such examination; the disciplinary power exercised by the EPI or the EPO in respect of professional representatives; and also the obligation of confidentiality on the professional representative and the privilege from disclosure in proceedings before the EPO in respect of communications with clients or any other persons.

617. it is to be noted that, contrary to the situation with professional representatives, legal practitioners entitled to act as representatives before the EPO are not entered on the list of professional representatives.[335]

618. Currently, the EPI has about 11,600 European patent attorneys as members coming from each of the thirty-eight Contracting States because, as explained, EPI membership is mandatory for all European patent attorneys. The EPO website includes an up-to-date database of professional representatives before the EPO as per the physical register located in their offices.

333. EPO CA/D 18/06.
334. EPC Art. 134a.
335. J 18/99 from 1 Oct. 2002, Reasons 5.2.

§9. Impact on National Law

619. As has been already presented, between the European patent system and the national one, specific to each and every EPC Member State, there is a 'peaceful coexistence' which nevertheless does not exclude significant mutual influence.

620. Impact of national law on EPC resides rather in bringing and integrating into the European system of the most valuable and largely harmonized national principles of examining work and legal procedures.

621. On the other side, the impact of the EPC on national law derives mostly from the internal mechanism of this convention, which involves that the European patent application and the patents granted thereof have the same value as the national ones in designated countries which leads to bundles of national patents in those countries which validated European patents.

622. Correspondingly, there are some main impact points which are referring to:

- Conversion into national patent applications.
- Revocation of European patents.
- Prior rights.
- Relation with national utility models.
- Payment of renewal fees.

and which will be further discussed.

I. Conversion into a National Patent Application

623. The equivalence of a European filing with a national filing enables providing, within the EPC,[336] of a 'conversion procedure' which can be initiated by a request for conversion made by the applicant.

624. According to this procedure, the Patent Office of a designated Contracting State may apply the procedure for the grant of a national patent at the request of the applicant for or proprietor of a European patent, in the following circumstances:

(a) where the application is deemed to be withdrawn pursuant to Article 77(3) EPC due to a possible delay by national authorities in forwarding the European application;
(b) in such other cases as are provided for by the national law in which the European patent application is refused or withdrawn or deemed to be withdrawn, or the European patent is revoked under the EPC.

336. EPC Art. 135 and Art. 137.

625. The request for conversion must be filed within three months after the date on which:

(a) the European patent application has been withdrawn;
(b) a communication has been notified that the application is deemed to be withdrawn; or
(c) a decision has been notified refusing the application or revoking the European patent.

626. The equivalence of the European patent to a regular national filing lapses if the request is not filed in due time.[337]

627. As a rule, the request for conversion must be filed with the EPO subject to a conversion fee to be been paid to the office and in this situation, the requests for conversion have to be transmitted by the office to the Patent Offices of the Contracting States specified therein accompanied by a copy of the files relating to the European patent application or the European patent.

628. However, if the applicant has been notified that the European patent application is deemed to be withdrawn, pursuant to Article 77(3) EPC, the request must be filed with the central industrial property office with which the application was filed. Where the request for conversion has to be filed with an NPO, that office, subject to the provisions of national security, transmits the request, together with a copy of the European patent application, directly to the central industrial property offices of the Contracting States specified by the applicant in the request. The equivalence of the European patent application to a regular national filing in the Contracting States designated lapses if the request for conversion is not transmitted within twenty months after the date of filing or date of priority.[338]

629. A transmitted European patent application shall not be subjected to formal requirements of national law which are different from or additional to those provided for in this convention.

630. Any NPO to which the European patent application is transmitted may require that the applicant shall, within a period of not less than two months:

(a) pay the national application fee; and
(b) file a translation of the original text of the European patent application in an official language of the state in question and, where appropriate, of the text as amended during proceedings before the EPO which the applicant wishes to use as the basis for the national procedure.

337. EPC Rule 155(1).
338. EPC Rule 155(3).

II. Revocation of European Patents

631. Revocation of a European patent has effect for all Contracting States where it has been validated and the procedure may be initiated only on the grounds that:[339]

- the subject matter of the European patent is not patentable;
- the European patent does not disclose the invention in a manner sufficiently clear and complete for it to be carried out by a person skilled in the art;
- the subject matter of the European patent extends beyond the content of the application as filed or, if the patent was granted on a divisional application or on a new application, beyond the content of the earlier application as filed;
- the protection conferred by the European patent has been extended; or
- the proprietor of the European patent is not entitled.

632. If the grounds for revocation affect the European patent only in part, the patent shall be limited by a corresponding amendment of the claims and revoked in part.

633. The wording of Article 138(2) clearly indicates that limitation and partial revocation of a European patent are always to take the form of a corresponding amendment to the patent claims, a partial revocation simply by amending the description or drawings being anymore possible.

634. In proceedings relating to the validity of the European patent, the proprietor of the patent shall have the right to limit the patent by amending the claims, the patent as thus limited, forming the basis for the proceedings.

635. This provision gives[340] the patent proprietor the right in such proceedings to submit an amended, that is, limited, version of his claims which, in his view, meets the objections to the validity of his patent. This limited version of the patent must then form the basis for subsequent proceedings. If the court or authority dealing with the case considers that the proprietor's own limitation is insufficient, it may further limit the patent or revoke it in full.

III. Prior Rights

636. A European patent application and a European patent designating a Contracting State and respectively a national patent application and a national patent in that Contracting State referring to the same invention, are enjoying the same prior right effect

339. EPC Art. 138.
340. EPO CA/PL 25/00 Rev. 1; Basic Proposal for the Revision of the European Patent Convention; Munich, 28.07.2000.

637. This means that[341] in any designated Contracting State a European patent application and a European patent shall have, with regard to a national patent application and a national patent, the same prior right effect as a national patent application and a national patent, and reciprocally, a national patent application and a national patent in a Contracting State shall have, with regard to a European patent designating that Contracting State, the same prior right effect as if the European patent were a national patent.

638. Regulation of the possible double protection is left by EPC to national legislation when providing that 'any Contracting State may prescribe whether and on what terms an invention disclosed in both a European patent application or patent and a national application or patent having the same date of filing or, where priority is claimed, the same date of priority, may be protected simultaneously by both applications or patents'.

IV. Other Effects

639. A first additional effect concerns registered utility models protection where relevant provisions on conversion and prior rights shall apply *mutatis mutandis* to utility models and utility certificates and to applications for utility models and utility certificates registered or deposited in the Contracting States whose laws make provision for such models or certificates.

640. Due to the fact that on the one side, renewal fees for the European patent application are to be paid directly to the EPO but the renewal fees for European patents are to be paid to the NPOs and 50% from them delivered to the EPO; EPC provides clear rules for managing renewal fees.[342]

641. Accordingly, renewal fees for a European patent may only be imposed for the years which follow the year in which the mention of the grant of the European patent is published in the European Patent Bulletin. Any renewal fees falling due within two months of the publication in the European Patent Bulletin of the mention of the grant of the European patent shall be deemed to have been validly paid if they are paid within that period, possible additional fees provided for under national law being excluded by EPC.

§10. Special Agreements

642. In its Part IX – Special agreements, EPC provides two types of 'special agreements', namely: on 'unitary patents' and respectively on 'other agreements between the Contracting States'.

---

341. EPC Art. 139.
342. EPC Art. 141.

643. Both of them received in the period following the revision year 2000, a particular focus due to the strong developments aiming at enacting and enforcing at the level of most European countries on one side of a strong patent system with unitary effect, including its dedicated jurisdiction and on the other side, to implement a more efficient and cost-effective patent system.

I. Provision on Unitary Patents

644. EPC provides explicitly that a/any group of Contracting States may conclude by a special agreement that a European patent granted for those states has a unitary character throughout their territories and the European patent may only be granted jointly in respect of all these states.[343]

645. The group of Contracting States may give additional tasks to the EPO[344] which, in order to be carried out, could lead to the setting up of special departments common to the Contracting States within the European office, directed by the President.

646. The group of Contracting States may lay down special provisions to govern representation of parties before the departments.[345]

647. In the working mechanism of the Unitary Patent system, an extremely important piece is represented by the Select Committee of the AC which, according to the EPC, may be set by the group of Contracting States[346] for the purpose of supervising the activities of the special departments. The EPO has to put at its disposal, the necessary staff, premises, and equipment for the performance of its duties.

648. The composition, powers, and functions of the Select Committee are determined by the group of Contracting States.

649. For further details on the current structure and the task entrusted, please refer to Chapter 5 §3 II.

650. Covering for expenditure and expenses for carrying out special tasks given to the EPO comes in the charge of the group of Contracting States, including the expenditure on staff, premises, and equipment chargeable in respect of these specific departments.

651. Mentioned rules are incorporating and extending relevant EPC articles dedicated to unitary patent.

343. EPC Art. 142.
344. EPC Art. 143.
345. EPC Art. 144.
346. EPC Art. 145; However, the legal basis for the Select Committee lies not only in the Art. 145 EPC but also in the Art. 9(2) of Regulation (EU) No 1257/2012.

652. Renewal fees for unitary patents[347] are to be paid in the proportion established for classical European patents (currently 50% for the EPO) subject to the normal condition that the group of Contracting States has fixed a common scale of renewal fees in respect of European patents and Rules relating to Fees for UPP are establishing exactly this scheme of renewal fees.

653. EPC gives the freedom to the group of Contracting States to provide that[348] a European patent application for which these Contracting States are designated may only be transferred, mortgaged, or subjected to any legal means of execution in respect of all the Contracting States of the group and in accordance with the provisions of the special agreement.

654. A specific article dedicated to joint designation[349] provides a joint designation for both European patent applications as well as for PCT applications where the EPO acts as a designated office.

655. For the first situation, 'the group of Contracting States may provide that these states may only be designated jointly and that the designation of only one or some of such states shall be deemed to constitute the designation of all the states of the group' and for other situations 'where the EPO acts as a designated office designation applies if the applicant has indicated in the international application that he wishes to obtain a European patent for one or more of the designated states of the group. The same shall apply if the applicant designates in the international application one of the Contracting States in the group, whose national law provides that the designation of that state shall have the effect of the application being for a European patent'.

II. Other Agreements Between the Contracting States

656. As mentioned in Chapter 2 §4, the EPC 2000 enacted the new Article 149a entitled 'other agreements between the Contracting States' which made possible the conclusion of the London Agreement – detailed in Chapter 5 §2 and of the EPLA agreement – detailed in Chapter 5 §4.

657. It provides[350] in this respect that:

(1) Nothing in this Convention shall be construed as limiting the right of some or all of the Contracting States to conclude special agreements on any matters concerning European patent applications or European patents which under this Convention are subject to and governed by national law, such as, in particular:

347. EPC Art. 147.
348. EPC Art. 148.
349. EPC Art. 149.
350. EPC Art. 149 a.

(a) an agreement establishing a European Patent Court common to the Contracting States party to it;
(b) an agreement establishing an entity common to the Contracting States party to it to deliver, at the request of national courts or quasi-judicial authorities, opinions on issues of European or harmonized national patent law;
(c) an agreement under which the Contracting States party to it dispense fully or in part with translations of European patents under Article 65;
(d) an agreement under which the Contracting States party to it provide that translations of European patents as required under Article 65 may be filed with, and published by, the European Patent Office.

(2) The AC shall be competent to decide that:
(a) the members of the Boards of Appeal or the Enlarged Board of Appeal may serve on a European Patent Court or a common entity and take part in proceedings before that court or entity in accordance with any such agreement;
(b) the European Patent Office shall provide a common entity with such support staff, premises and equipment as may be necessary for the performance of its duties, and the expenses incurred by that entity shall be borne fully or in part by the organization.

658. Article 149a(1) expressly underlines that the convention does not prevent any Contracting State from concluding with other Contracting States, agreements on any matters which under the EPC are governed by national law.[351]

659. Sublist (a) and (b) are clearly addressed to the EPLA and respectively, sublist (c) and (d) to the London Agreement.

660. Article 149a(2) addresses the involvement of the EPOrg in the implementation of the said agreements.

661. Its provision leaves the members of EPO Boards of Appeal free to serve on the European Patent Court and/or common entity while continuing to serve on the Boards of Appeal. It offers a clear legal basis in the EPC enabling the AC to decide that the members of the boards are entitled to do so.

662. It also offers a clear legal basis in the EPC enabling the AC to decide that the EPO provides the common entity with the necessary staff, premises, and equipment and that the expenses incurred by such an entity be borne fully or in part by the EPOrg.

351. EPC Art. 2, Art. 64(2)and Art. 65.

§11. International Applications Under the PCT

663. Part X of the EPC[352] forms the legal basis for all EPO activities under the PCT and is intended for applicants seeking worldwide patent protection by using the services of the EPO under the PCT, in such a way that the PCT applications may be filed, searched and examined at the EPO.

664. Generally, this procedure is called EURO-PCT route of the patent protection.

665. International applications filed under the PCT may be the subject of proceedings before the EPO, where the provisions of the PCT and its Regulations shall be applied supplemented by the provisions of the EPC. In case of conflict, the provisions of the PCT or its Regulations prevail.

666. EPC provides explicitly that within the EURO-PCT procedure, the EPO may act as a receiving Office, as an ISA or International Preliminary Examining Authority (IPEA), and also as designated Office or elected Office.

667. The PCT does not expressly provide for appeal or petition during the international phase but there is, however, a single exception under the EPC[353] on the boards' competence to decide on protests against additional search or examination fees charged by the EPO acting as ISA or IPEA after a finding of lack of unity of

668. Where acting as an ISA and IPEA, it is allowed, in principle, for applicants who are residents or nationals of a state party to the EPC but a possible flexibility for other applicants within a specific agreement (EPO-WIPO).

669. The EPO may be a designated office for any state party to the EPC in respect of which the PCT is in force which is designated in the international application and for which the applicant wishes to obtain a European patent, and may be an elected Office, if the applicant has elected a state previously designated.

670. Those international applications for which EPO is a designated or elected Office and which has been accorded an international date of filing are equivalent to a regular European application (EURO-PCT application).

671. The international publication of a EURO-PCT application in an official language of the EPO. It takes the place of the publication of the European patent application and shall be mentioned in the European Patent Bulletin.

672. If the EURO-PCT application is published in another language, a translation into one of the official languages shall be filed with the EPO, which it publishes and starting with that date, the provisional protection becomes effective.

352. EPC Art. 150–Art. 153.
353. EPO-Case Law of the Boards of Appeal; VI 2; 8th edition, July 2016.

673. It should be obvious that the EURO-PCT application is treated as a European patent application and consequently considered as comprised in the state of the art.

674. The international search report drawn up in respect of a EURO-PCT application or the declaration replacing it and their international publication normally takes the place of the European search report and the mention of its publication in the European Patent Bulletin.

675. Once the EURO-PCT application enters the regional phase before the EPO, the appeal procedures provided for under the EPC supplement the provisions of the PCT.[354]

676. There are thus the following possibilities[355] for a European application filed under the provisions of the PCT:

(i) the filing of the application and the international search take place at an office or offices other than the EPO. The EPO is a designated Office;
(ii) the application is filed at another office but the EPO performs the international search. The EPO acts as ISA and is a designated Office;
(iii) the application is filed at the EPO, which also performs the international search. The EPO acts as receiving Office, ISA and designated Office;
(iv) in addition to the cases mentioned under (1)–(3), the applicant files a demand for international preliminary examination. The EPO is the 'elected Office';
(v) the EPO is the IPEA. It may carry out this function without being the receiving Office, a designated Office or an elected Office. The EPO can, however, only act as an IPEA if the international search was carried out by the EPO, the Austrian, Spanish, Swedish, Finnish, or Turkish Patent Office, the NPI or the Visegrad Patent Institute;
(vi) if the international search has been carried out by an office other than the EPO, the applicant may still request the EPO to perform a Supplementary International Search (SIS) in its capacity as Supplementary International Search Authority (SISA).

§12. Transitional and Final Provisions

677. A complete panorama of the EPC makes a short presentation of these last type of administrative provisions necessary indeed, although on one side, the transitional provisions have been deleted during the revisions process and the final ones remained practically unchanged and somehow lost the substance of their importance Article 164 EPC brings the necessary clarification that the Implementing

354. J 20/89, OJ 1991.
355. EPO EURO-PCT Guide; PCT Procedure at the EPO ; Guide for Applicants; A 10th edition Updated January 2017.

Regulations, the Protocol on Recognition, the Protocol on Privileges and Immunities, the Protocol on Centralisation, the Protocol on the Interpretation of Article 69 and the Protocol on Staff Complement, all of which we are referring in Chapter 4, are integral parts of the convention, its provisions prevailing in case of conflict with those of the Implementing Regulations.

678. Outside the thirty-eight states which are currently EPC members and which joined this convention either as founding members or following an acceding process (*see* Chapter 3 §3 I), accession to the EPC[356] is opened to any other European State at the invitation of the AC or to any state which has ceased to be a party to the convention and wishes again 'to join the club', accession being instrumented with the Government of the Federal Republic of Germany.

679. However, the neutral expression 'at the invitation of the Administrative Council' should be indeed understood in this process as a deep and strong political and legal opinion expressed by its members on the current situation in the candidate country.

680. For Contracting States with particular constitutional and administrative situations where they are responsible for external relations of one or more territories, it is provided [357] their possibility to declare adequately or to make a written notification that EPC is applicable to one or more of the territories for the external relations of which it is responsible, European patents granted for that Contracting State having a direct effect in these territories. Contrarily, those Contracting States may, at any time, declare that the convention shall cease to apply to some or to all of the territories in respect of which it has given notification.

681. Following Article 169, for Belgium, Germany, France, Luxembourg, Netherlands, Switzerland, and the UK, the EPC entered into force on 7 October 1977

682. However, any ratification or accession of other Contracting States after the entry into force of the EPC took effect on the first day of the third month after the deposit of the instrument of ratification or accession.

683. Any state which ratifies or accedes to the EPC after its entry into force must pay to the EPOrg an initial non-refundable contribution[358] of 5% of an amount calculated by applying the percentage obtained for the state in question on the date on which ratification or accession takes effect, in accordance with the scale provided, to the sum of the special financial contributions due from the other Contracting States in respect of the accounting periods preceding the date referred to above.

356. EPC Art. 166.
357. EPC Art. 168.
358. EPC Art. 170.

684. EPC has provided an unlimited duration[359] but, any Contracting State may at any time, denounce it; denunciation being notified to the Government of the Federal Republic of Germany and taking effect one year after the date of receipt of such notification.

685. According to Article 172, EPC may be revised by a conference of the Contracting States, prepared and convened by the AC. The conference is validly constituted only with a representation of at least three-quarters of the Contracting States. Adoption of the revised text requires again, a majority of three-quarters of the Contracting States represented and voting at the conference, abstentions being considered as votes.

686. The revised text must enter into force when it has been ratified or acceded to by the number of Contracting States specified by the conference and at the time specified by that conference. Those states that have not ratified or acceded to the revised text of the convention at the time of its entry into force shall cease to be parties to the EPC as from that time.

687. Finally, disputes between Contracting States[360] concerning the interpretation or application of the EPC which is not settled by negotiation must be submitted at the request of one of the states concerned, to the AC, which shall endeavour to bring about an agreement between the states concerned, and if it is not reached within six months, any one of the states concerned may submit the dispute to the International Court of Justice for a binding decision

359. EPC Art. 171 and Art. 174.
360. EPC Art. 173.

Chapter 4. Additional Texts

§1. General Considerations

688. This chapter is intended for a concise presentation and interpretation of all those texts which are considered 'additional', however, according to Article 164(1) EPC, they are integral parts of the EPC.

§2. Implementing Regulations

I. General Aspects

689. The official text is that of the Implementing Regulations to the convention on the Grant of European Patents of 5 October 1973 as adopted by the decision of the AC on 7 December 2006 and as last amended by decision of the AC on 14 October 2015.

690. The function of the Implementing Regulations is 'to determine in more detail how the Articles should be applied and there is nothing in the convention allowing the conclusion that this would not also apply in the case of Articles governing issues of substantive patent law.'[361]

691. According to Article 164(2), 'in case of conflict between the provisions of this convention and those of the Implementing Regulations, the provisions of this convention shall prevail'.

692. In the last two decades, the EPC Implementing Regulations suffered important revisions – sometimes called 'complete overhaul[362]' – of the Articles of the EPC.

693. This overhaul has been carried out in two stages:

- Following the results of the Diplomatic Conference in November 2000, new Implementing Regulations to the EPC 2000 were adopted by the AC on 12 December 2002.
- Considering that amendments of the Implementing Regulations to the EPC 2000 were necessary and useful in the light of more recent developments, the AC amended the Implementing Regulations to the EPC 2000 on 7 December 2006.

694. Remembering that one of the targets of the EPC 2000 was a certain 'flexibility through deregulation'(*see* Chapter 2 §5) by shifting many provisions from the

361. G 2/07, OJ 2012.
362. EPO- Implementing Regulations to the EPC 2000; https://www.epo.org/law-practice/legal-texts/epc/archive/documentation/implementing-regulations.html.

body of the convention to the Implementing Regulations to authorize future modifications by the AC, it is clear that by this movement, the EPC Implementing Regulations increased substantially their importance.

695. Relevant provisions have been already presented and commented, whenever was necessary, in detail of the related EPC articles.

§3. Protocol on Recognition

I. General Aspects

696. We are referring here to the Protocol on Jurisdiction and the Recognition of Decisions in respect of the Right to the Grant of a European Patent of 5 October 1973

697. Its object is to define which courts of the EPC Contracting States shall have jurisdiction to decide claims against the applicant, to the right to the grant of a European patent.

698. This protocol may be viewed as a core mechanism in the implementation and enforcement of a real European patent based on the recognition of the final decisions given in any Contracting State on the right to the grant of a European patent in respect of one or more of the Contracting States designated in the European patent application without requiring a special procedure in the other Contracting States.

699. Therefore, it represents, in fact, an implementation of Article 60 EPC on the right to a European patent by governing the competences of the national courts and recognition of their decisions in dealing with cases on that right.

700. It is self-explanatory that, as related to the right to the grant, this protocol applies only to European patent applications and not to the related granted patents.

II. Substantive Provisions

701. Recognition is made under some significant conditions:[363]

- the courts of the Contracting States have jurisdiction to decide claims against the applicant, to the right to the grant of a European patent in respect of one or more of the Contracting States designated in the European patent application;
- the jurisdiction of the court whose decision is to be recognized and the validity of such decision may not be reviewed;

363. Art.1, 9 and 11 Protocol on Recognition.

– in relations between any Contracting States, the provisions of the Protocol prevail over any conflicting provisions of other agreements on jurisdiction or the recognition of judgments.

702. The Protocol provides[364] distinct geographical allocations of jurisdiction depending on the situations where:

– if an applicant for a European patent has his/her residence or principal place of business within one of the Contracting States, proceedings shall be brought against him/her in the courts of that Contracting State;
– if an applicant for a European patent has his residence or principal place of business outside the Contracting States and if the party claiming the right to the grant of the European patent has his/her residence or principal place of business within one of the Contracting States, the courts of the latter state shall have exclusive jurisdiction;
– if the subject matter of a European patent application is an employee's invention, the courts of the Contracting State, if any, whose law determines the right to the European patent, has exclusive jurisdiction over proceedings between the employee and the employer;
– if the parties to a dispute concerning the right to the grant of a European patent are bounded by an agreement providing which court decides on such a dispute, that court has exclusive jurisdiction.

703. The courts of the Federal Republic of Germany have exclusive jurisdiction in all other cases.

704. Anyway, the courts of Contracting States before which claims are brought decides on their own motion, whether or not they have jurisdiction.

705. Finally, the protocol provides[365] a chronological allocation of jurisdiction depending on the situations where:

– If proceedings based on the same claim and between the same parties are brought before courts of different Contracting States, the court to which a later application is made shall on its own motion decline jurisdiction in favour of the court to which an earlier application was made.
– The jurisdiction of the court to which an earlier application is made was challenged, the court to which a later application is made stays the proceedings until the other court takes a final decision.

364. Art.2 3, 4, 5 and 6 Protocol on Recognition.
365. Art.7, 8 Protocol on Recognition.

§4. Protocol on Privileges and Immunities

I. General Aspects

706. Officially, it is recognized as the Protocol on Privileges and Immunities of the EPOrg of 5 October 1973 and it defines[366] the immunity of the EPOrg staff and the inviolability of its premises ensuring thus, that the activity of the Organization is not restricted in performing its task by domestic law.

707. According to Article 8 EPC, this Protocol must define the conditions under which the EPOrg, the members of the AC, the employees of the EPO, and other persons involved in the work of the EPOrg are enjoying, in each Contracting State, the privileges and immunities necessary for the performance of their duties.

708. Its provisions are largely common to all big international organizations and are covering some basic points.

II. Basic Provisions

709. The first stipulated principle refers to the inviolability[367] of the:

- premises of the EPOrg;
- archives of the EPOrg and any documents belonging to or held by it.

710. The second one covers immunity[368] in the sense that:

- within the scope of its official activities and subject to some particular exceptions, the organization shall have immunity from jurisdiction and execution;
- the property and assets of the organization, wherever situated, are immune from any form of requisition, confiscation, expropriation, sequestration, administrative or provisional judicial constraint.

711. The main part of the Protocol covers[369] the privileges and immunities themselves of the:

- representatives of Contracting States, alternate Representatives and their advisers or experts;
- representatives of foreign governments on temporary official missions;

366. Visser Derek –The Annotated European Patent Convention, pg. 14; 21 revised edition. H.TEL, Publisher 2013.
367. Art. 1, 2 Protocol on Privileges and Immunities.
368. Art. 3 Protocol on Privileges and Immunities.
369. Art. 12, 13, 14, 15 Protocol on Privileges and Immunities.

- President of the EPO who enjoys the privileges and immunities accorded to diplomatic agents under the Vienna Convention on Diplomatic Relations of 18 April 1961;
- employees of the EPO: the AC may decide the categories of employees to whom the provisions of privileges and immunities applies but the President of the EPO has the duty to waive immunity where he considers that such immunity prevents the normal course of justice;
- experts performing functions on behalf of or carrying out missions for the EPOrg;

712. Finally, the Protocol provides[370] internal privileged taxation policy of the EPOrg which refers to:

- exemption from all direct taxes for the EPOrg and its property and income within the scope of its official activities;
- exemption from duties and charges on import or export other than fees or taxes representing services rendered, for goods imported or exported by the EPOrg for the exercise of its official activities;
- internal taxation of the relevant staff of the EPO and consequently, exemption from all compulsory contributions to national social security schemes subject to the agreements made with the Contracting States.

§5. Protocol on the Centralisation

I. General Aspects

713. We are referring here to the Protocol on the Centralization of the European Patent System (PCen) and its introduction on 5 October 1973. as revised by the Act revising the EPC of 29 November 2000.

714. The PCen had from the very beginning, two main tasks in providing a clear working mechanism for the centralized patenting procedure ensured by the EPO namely:

- ensuring an initial smooth transfer from the International Patent Institute set up by the Hague Agreement of 6 June 1947, to the EPO (*see* Chapter 1 §1);
- unambiguous allocation of tasks between the EPO with its centralized patenting procedure including the EURO-PCT one, and the NPOs of the activities as IPEA and ISA under the PCT general procedure.

715. Provisions covering the first task have, for the time being, only a historical meaning.

370. Art. 4 to 9, 16 Protocol on Privileges and Immunities.

716. Regarding allocations of tasks within PCT procedures, this Protocol consecrates the centralization principle which provides[371] that as a matter of fact, the EPC Member States renounce, on behalf of their central industrial property offices, in favour of the EPO, any activities as ISA and as IPEA under the PCT.

II. Main Provisions

717. This Protocol offers[372] a relevant derogation from the centralization principle for the Patent Offices of those Member States in which the official language is not one of the official languages of the EPO and which may, however, be authorized to act as an ISA and as an IPEA under the PCT. Such authorization includes the restriction for the state concerned to limit activities to international applications filed by nationals or residents of such state and by nationals or residents of states parties to the EPC which are adjacent to that state. By decision of the AC, the central industrial property office of any state party to the convention may be allowed to extend such activities to cover such international applications as may be filed by nationals or residents of any non-Contracting State having the same official language as the Contracting State in question and drawn up in that language.

718. Provided is a mechanism of harmonizing the search activities under the PCT within the framework of the European patent system between the EPO and the authorized industrial property by intensive cooperation.

719. The PCen made possible that exactly on 1 January 2017, the EPO; the Austrian, Finnish, Spanish, and Swedish Patent Offices; as well as the NPI and the Visegrad Patent Institute were acting as European ISAs and IPEAs.[373]

720. The NPI is an intergovernmental organization which acts, among other tasks, as an ISA and Preliminary Examination Authority under the PCT system for nationals and residents of Denmark, Iceland, Norway, and Sweden. Since 1 January 2008, the Institute acts as PCT Authority and as of 1 May 2013, it is, with the EPO and the Swedish Patent and Registration Office, one of the three ISAs and IPEAs available for international applications filed with the receiving Offices of Denmark, Iceland, Norway, and Sweden.

721. The Visegrad Patent Institute follows, as a matter of fact, the institutional lines set up by the NPI and acts as an intergovernmental organization for cooperation in the field of patents created by the NPOs of the four Visegrad countries, namely: the Czech Republic, Hungary, Poland, and Slovakia. The Institute aims at operating as an ISA and IPEA under the PCT as from 1 July 2016

371. Section I(2) Protocol on Centralisation.
372. Section III(1) and (2) Protocol on Centralisation.
373. EPO- Guide for applicants: PCT procedure before the EPO (EURO-PCT Guide) CI, para.200–201.

722. It should be kept in mind that according to the centralization procedure, the EPO acts as an IPEA only if the international search was carried out by the EPO itself or by another European ISA.

723. The Protocol under analysis provides[374] a further flexibility of the centralization principle when allowing, by decision of the AC, for the purpose of facilitating the adaptation of the NPOs of the EPC Member States parties to the EPC, to entrust the central industrial property offices of such of those states in which it is possible to conduct the proceedings in one of the official languages of the EPO with tasks concerning the examination of European patent applications drawn up in that language. Such tasks shall be carried out within the framework of the proceedings for grant laid down in the EPC.

724. The entrusted tasks may not, however, extend over provided limits.

725. Also, it is provided that if the AC considers that it is compatible with the proper functioning of the EPO, it may entrust searching in respect of European patent applications to the central industrial property offices of those states in which the official language is one of the official languages of the EPO, provided that these offices possess the necessary qualifications for appointment as an ISA in accordance with the conditions laid down in the PCT.

726. The AC may also extend, under provided conditions, the authorizations to the central industrial property office of a Contracting State which does not have as an official language one of the official languages of the EPO.

727. The decisions of the AC provided for in this Protocol require a three-quarters majority.

§6. Protocol on the Interpretation of Article 69 of the Convention

I. General Aspects

728. As already indicated, we are referring here to the text of the Protocol on the Interpretation of Article 69 EPC of 5 October 1973 as revised by the Act revising the EPC of 29 November 2000.

729. Article 69 covers one of the most important substantive provisions of the EPC when stipulating that the extent of the protection conferred by a European patent or a European patent application is determined by the claims which in their turn are to be interpreted by the description and, as the case might be, by drawings.

374. Section IV Protocol on Centralisation.

730. Even from its beginning in EPC 1973, the Protocol attempted to harmonize two different interpretation traditions in Europe – on the one hand, the British tradition which attaches particular importance to the wording of the patent claims which naturally leads to a due consideration for third-party interests; and on the other hand, the continental tradition which is more oriented on the inventive concept expressed in the patent document, and which is rather oriented towards the interests of the patentee. The Protocol has had a considerable effect at national level and has in this way contributed to the harmonization of patent law in Europe.

II. Basic Provisions

731. The attempt on harmonization is consistent with Article 1 on General principles which originates in the original form of the EPC 1973, and provides that:

> Article 69 should not be interpreted as meaning that the extent of the protection conferred by a European patent is to be understood as that defined by the strict, literal meaning of the wording used in the claims, the description and drawings being employed only for the purpose of resolving an ambiguity found in the claims. Nor should it be taken to mean that the claims serve only as a guideline and that the current protection conferred may extend to what, from a consideration of the description and drawings by a person skilled in the art, the patent proprietor has contemplated. On the contrary, it is to be interpreted as defining a position between these extremes which combines a fair protection for the patent proprietor with a reasonable degree of legal certainty for third parties.

732. Article 2 has been introduced by the Diplomatic Conference from 2000 (*see* Chapter 2 §3 D) and is aimed at recognizing and introducing, in fact, the doctrine of equivalents in the examination of the extent of protection conferred by European patents, and provides that:

> For the purpose of determining the extent of protection conferred by a European patent, due account shall be taken of any element which is equivalent to an element specified in the claims.

733. This provision offers the basic principle for an extended patent claim interpretation with the so-called doctrine of equivalence according to which, the extent or scope of protection is not limited to the identical use of the features given in the claim but also extends to equivalent embodiments, subject to the condition that the person skilled in the art is able to understand the latter as being equally effective.

734. However, the intended definition of an 'equivalent means' contained in the draft proposal of the EPC 2000:[375]

375. EPO CA/100/00 e; Basic Proposal for the Revision of the European Patent Convention.

> A means shall generally be considered as being equivalent if it would be obvious to a person skilled in the art that using such means would achieve substantially the same result as that achieved through the means specified in the claim

has been rejected and therefore the definition of an equivalent element/mean is left at the interpretation of national courts.

735. Anyway, the Protocol provides clearly that the scope of protection of a patent also embraces embodiments which are covered by the 'terms' of the claims to be determined by interpretation.

736. The scope of protection is exclusively determined by the terms of the claims and the extent of the inventive idea which has found expression in the patent claims. Thus, the scope of protection according to Article 69 EPC is not restricted to the wording of the patent claims but is defined by their 'terms' which have to be determined by finding a possible equivalence between the infringement form and the patented subject matter.

737. It is taken into consideration that the evaluation is made by a skilled person's knowledge at the priority date of the patent in suit.

738. The person skilled in the art which has the task to interpret the terms of the claims is, in principle, the same as that for assessing inventive step[376] (*see* Chapter 4 §4 II B 3).

739. In the continental approach, equivalence is evaluated by[377] comparing the function of the features of the patent claim which contribute to the solution of the technical problem of the patent in suit with the function of the features of the infringement form. Here, the decisive question is whether the skilled person having knowledge of the claimed invention will be able to solve the technical problem underlying the patented invention with modified but equivalent means, that is, whether he/she will arrive at the desired result with other (modified) means which also lead to the desired result.

740. It is considered[378] that, outside common principles of solving the technical problem by a technical solution between the granted patent and invention supposed to infringe that patent, there is no equivalence. Consequently, at a different posing of the technical problem, a possible equivalence should not be confirmed.

---

376. Strenc, Alexandru, Bucura Ionescu & Gheorghe Gheorghiu.Treaty on Patent Law.pg. 275 Editura Lumina Lex, 2007.
377. Tauchner Paul- The Principles of the Doctrine of Equivalence in Germany; http://www.vossiusandpartner.com/fileadmin/Redakteure/Archiv/2000_The_Principles_of_the_Doctrine_of.pdf.
378. Benckard Georg – Patentgesetz & Gebrauchsmustergesetz, pg. 537; C.H.Beck'sche Verlagsbuchhandlung, München, 1993.

741. Finally, the concept of 'success' might have significance in judging equivalence where is considered that [379] 'equivalence exists where for a unitary inventive concept are used equivalent means with practically same success'.

§7. Protocol on Staff Complement

742. The official name is the Protocol on the Staff Complement of the EPO at The Hague of 29 November 2000 and the text was adopted by the AC in its decision of 28 June 2001 and has become an integral part of the Revision Act of 29 November 2000 under Article 3(2), second sentence, of that Act.

743. This protocol is meant[380] to ensure the adequate proportion of EPO posts assigned to the duty station at The Hague comparing the general allocation of posts proven necessary for the proper functioning of the EPO. The final decision rests at the level of the AC on a proposal from the President of the EPO after consultation with the Governments of Germany and Netherlands.

379. *Ibid* pg. 537.
380. EPO CA/100/00 e; Basic Proposal for the Revision of The European Patent Convention.

Chapter 5. Relationship to Other International Conventions

§1. General Considerations

744. In previous chapters, the full compatibility of the current EPC with main international conventions and treaties have been detailed.

745. First, the EPC constitutes a special agreement within the meaning of Article 19 of the Paris Convention for the Protection of Industrial Property which stipulates that:

> It is understood that the countries of the Union reserve the right to make separately between themselves special agreements for the protection of industrial property, in so far as these agreements do not contravene the provisions of this Convention

746. This means that not only the general principles of the Paris Convention with regard to industrial property on claiming priority and the national treatment principle but also the specific provisions on patents equally apply in the European procedure and to European applications.

747. Chapter 2 §2 has detailed the manner by which relevant provisions of the TRIPS and PLT were implemented in the revised EPC.

748. There are, however, important legal, administrative, and procedural interconnections of the EPC with other international and European agreements,[381] specifically dedicated to patents, which need our further attention.

§2. Relationship with the PCT; the EURO-PCT Approach

749. Considerations made under this chapter are following two types of relationships between EPC and PCT that need to be further analysed, namely:

- direct implementation of the PCT in Part X of the EPC, summarized in Chapter 3 §11, and further developed;
- common or largely similar provisions on substantive patenting concepts and procedures for both international conventions.

381. EPO- Guide for applicants: How to Get a European patent; AIII.

I. EPC as Regional Patent Treaty Within the Meaning of PCT

A. Applicable Law

750. The key to this relationship is based on the fact that the EPC constitutes a regional patent treaty within the meaning of Article 45 PCT, which provides that:

(1) Any treaty providing for the grant of regional patents ('regional patent treaty'), and giving to all persons who, … .., are entitled to file international applications the right to file applications for such patents, may provide that international applications designating or electing a state party to both the regional patent treaty and the present Treaty may be filed as applications for such patents.
(2) The national law of the said designated or elected state may provide that any designation or election of such state in the international application shall have the effect of an indication of the wish to obtain a regional patent under the regional patent treaty.

751. It means that European patents can be granted by initiating European regional processing of an international (PCT) patent application at the EPO. This is called the 'EURO-PCT' route and the application is referred to as a 'EURO-PCT' application

752. The applicable law[382] in relationship PCT-EPC is to be found in the provisions of the PCT and its Regulations ('the PCT Rules') apply, supplemented by the provisions of Part X of the EPC, 'International applications under the Patent Cooperation Treaty – EURO-PCT applications', the Implementing Regulations to the EPC ('EPC Rules') and the relevant further legislation.

753. As a subsequent law in this matter, EPC provides that In case of conflict between the provisions of the EPC and those of the PCT or the PCT Rules, the PCT prevails. However, the EPO has withdrawn all notifications of incompatibility with PCT provisions, with effect from the entry into force of EPC 2000 on 13 December 2007.

754. In accordance with the principle of the prevalence of the PCT, applicants should refer[383] to the PCT International Search and Preliminary Examination Guidelines ('GL/ISPE', 'ISPE Guidelines') for information on search and examination practice and procedure before the EPO as ISA, SISA and IPEA, and in addition, are indeed applicable the PCT-EPO Guidelines but only to the extent that they can be applied in conformity with the supplementary role of the EPC in the international phase.

---

382. EPC Art. 150(2).
383. EPO- 'EURO-PCT Guide': PCT procedure at the EPO International phase and entry into the European phase Guide for applicants 10th edition Updated until 1 January 2017.

755. The agreement of October 2007 currently in force, last revised with effect from 1 January 2015, between the EPO and the International Bureau of WIPO ('Agreement EPO-WIPO')[384] concerning the functioning of the EPO as International Authority (ISA, SISA and IPEA) set out specific points of the work of the EPO in its PCT Authority duties.

B. EPO Tasks as PCT Authority

756. As presented in Chapter 3 §11, within this procedure, the EPO acts in its capacity as:

- a receiving Office;
- an ISA;
- an SISA;
- an IPEA; and/or
- a designated or elected Office.

757. Basic provisions of the mentioned EPO-WIPO Agreement could be summarized as follows:

(a) EPO carries out its activities as PCT Authority as are provided under the PCT, its Regulations, the Administrative Instructions and the Agreement, by applying and observing all the common rules of international search and of international preliminary examination, and understands its requirement to maintain a quality management system in compliance with the PCT requirements.
(b) The EPO acts as ISA for any international application filed with the receiving Office of, or acting for, any Contracting State, provided that the receiving Office specifies the EPC for that purpose, that such application, or a translation thereof furnished for the purposes of international search, is in the language or one of the specified languages, that such application is not an application of a kind specified, where applicable, that the EPC has been chosen by the applicant.
(c) The EPO acts as IPEA for any international application filed with the receiving Office of, or acting for, any Contracting State, provided that the receiving Office specifies the EPC for that purpose, that such application, or a translation thereof furnished for the purposes of international preliminary examination, is in the language or one of the accepted language, that such application is not an application of a specified kind specified and, where applicable, that the Authority has been chosen by the applicant; the following languages are accepted as the case might be: English, French, German, and, where the receiving Office is the industrial property office of Belgium or the Netherlands, Dutch.
(d) Where an international application is filed with the International Bureau as receiving Office, points (b) and (c) apply as if that application had been filed with a receiving competent Office.

---

384. OJ EPO 2010, 304, in consolidated version including amendments published in OJ EPO 2014, A117 and OJ EPO 2016, A30.

(e) The EPO conducts SISs covering the documents held in the search collection of the Authority, including, but not limited to the PCT minimum documentation.
(f) The EPO is not obliged to search any international application to the extent that it considers that such application relates to provided subject matter, with the exception of the subject matter (any subject matter) which is searched or examined under the EPC grant procedure.
(g) EPC functioning as a PCT Authority is based on an agreed schedule of fees and other charges which the EPO is entitled to make and a refund scheme is provided where the EPO reuse partially of totally previous done work or obtained results.
(h) Solely the symbols of International Patent Classification-IPC and in addition to it, the Cooperative Patent Classification (CPC) are to be indicated in the EPO produced specifications;
(i) Languages of Correspondence Used by the EPC will be English, French, or German, depending on the language in which the international application is filed or translated;
(j) The EPO agrees to carry out international-type searches to the extent decided by it.

758. Currently, the EPO is, in its quality as PCT Authority, one of the most preeminent worldwide actor, ranking :[385]

- 1st as ISA with approximately 81,000 ISRs established (about 40% of the worldwide number)
- 1st as IPEA with almost 8,000 International Preliminary Examination Reports (IPERs) (about 55% of the worldwide number), and
- 3rd as receiving Office with approximately 33,000 PCT applications (15.4% of all PCT applications filed)

II. Substantive Harmonization with EPC

759. EPO drafted a comprehensive list of harmonized provisions of the PCT and EPC [386] comprising equivalence tables between EPC Articles and Rules and related PCT Articles, which is further presented, together with our own comments covering each point of equivalence.

EPC	*PCT*	*Comment*
82	Rule 13.1	Identical formulation of the principle of the unity of invention

385. Niclas Morey, John Beatty- PCT Developments U.S. Bar -EPO Partnership for Quality meeting; 12 May 2015.
386. EPO- Guidelines for Search and Examination at the EPO as PCT Authority; 3.1 Annex I: EPC-PCT equivalence table.

EPC	*PCT*	*Comment*
83	5	Quasi-identical provision on the disclosure of the invention
84	6	Quasi-identical provision on claims
87, 88	8	Harmonized in substance provisions (based on PARIS Convention) on priority right and its claiming
128(1)	30	Harmonized provisions on unpublished applications not available for inspection
128(4)	Rule 94	Harmonized provisions on the possibility of inspection, on request and subject to the restrictions, after the publication of the relevant patent application, of the files relating to the application and the resulting patent
53(c)	Rules 39.1, 67.1	Coherent and harmonized provisions on the exceptions to patentability of the medical methods practised on the human or animal body
53(a)	Rule 9.1(i) (ii)	Provisions on inventions contrary to 'ordre public' or morality where: – EPC provides exclusion of the invention the commercial exploitation of which would be contrary to 'ordre public' or morality; – PCT provides that inventions must not contain expressions or drawings contrary to morality or to public order;
54(3)	Rules 64.3, 70.10	Harmonized provision on the inclusion within the state of the art in assessing novelty, the content of the patent applications as filed, with a prior date of filing and which were published on or after that date
55	Article 27(5) (6), Rule 4.17(v), Rule 51*bis*.1(a)(v)	Coherent provisions on non-prejudicial disclosures
54(1)	33(2)	Similar but coherent provision on novelty
54(2)	Rule 64	Similar but coherent provisions on the state of the art
56	33(3)	Quasi-identical provisions on inventive step

EPC	*PCT*	*Comment*
57	33(4)	Quasi-identical provisions on industrial applicability
67(1), (2), (3)	29(1), 29(2)	
123(2)	19(2), 34(2)(b)	Harmonized provisions on making amendments to the patent applications or related patents in proceedings before the Patent Office
53(b)	Rule 39.1(ii), Rule 67.1(ii)	Quasi-identical provisions on exceptions to patentability of the plant or animal varieties or essentially biological processes for the production of plants or animals

760. The extent of this photographic comparison lies outside the scope of this paper, but the underline of the most harmonized approaches on the substantive patent law indubitable indicates a relevant synergic approach between the two international treaties.

§3. Relation with the London Agreement[387]

761. Legal basis[388] for this agreement are to be found in Article 65(1) EPC(*see* Chapter 3) which states that any Contracting State may, if the European patent as granted, amended or limited by the EPO is not drawn up in one of its official languages, prescribe that the proprietor of the patent supply to its central industrial property office a translation of the patent as granted, amended, or limited in one of that state's official languages at his option or, where that state has prescribed the use of one specific official language, in that language.

762. The London Agreement is[389] an optional agreement aiming at reducing the costs relating to the translation of European patents by which the EPC Contracting States which have ratified or acceded to the agreement undertake to waive, entirely or largely, the requirement for translations of European patents.

763. The agreement resulted from a significant and longstanding endeavour of the EPOrg to reduce the costs of the post-grant translation regime based on the fact that on one side many Member States have official language/languages in common

387. Agreement on the application of Art. 65 of the Convention on the Grant of European Patents.
388. EPO- National Law relating to EPC; Chapt. IV. Translation requirements after grant.
389. EPO- Agreement on the application of Art. 65 EPC – London Agreement; www.epo.org/law-practice/legal-texts/london-agreement.html.

with the official languages of the EPO and on the other side, that some other Members States declared their readiness to renounce, at least partially, to translation requirements of the European patents into national language.

764. The basis of the process had been presented at the intergovernmental conference of the Member States of the EPOrg held in Paris on 24–25 June 1999 at the invitation of the French Government.[390] The conference adopted a mandate setting up two working parties with the task of submitting reports to the governments of the Contracting States on reducing the cost of European patents, a task which led to the London Agreement, and that of harmonizing patent litigations which led to the proposed EPLA, which will be later presented.

765. The working party on translation regime was instructed to draft[391] an 'optional protocol to the EPC, under which its signatory states undertake not to require the translation of the description of the European patent, provided that it is available in English ... [or alternatively] provided that it is available in one of the official EPO languages as designated by each signatory state'.

766. The London Agreement was concluded at the intergovernmental conference held in the London on 17 October 2000[392] to lower the translation costs faced by patent proprietors.[393] It is to be noted that the initial aim expressed by the Paris Intergovernmental Conference to conclude a 'protocol', was raised at the level of 'agreement' thus, legally and practically increasing its substance and importance,

767. Having in view that more states became party to the London Agreement increased the hope that patent proprietors will request and validate their patents in a greater number of states and thus reducing the pressure of known problem of prohibitive translation costs for European patents.

768. The main benefit is expected to come for prolific inventors and companies with strong patenting activity and effectively for the European industry and economy.

769. According to the provisions of the said agreement, the EPC Contracting States which are parties to the agreement undertake to waive, entirely or largely, the requirement for translations of European patents, as follows:

(a) a state which has an official language in common with one of the official languages of the EPO shall dispense entirely with the translation requirements provided for in Article 65(1) EPC;

390. Intergovernmental conference of the Member States of the European Patent Organisation on the reform of the patent system in Europe, Paris, 24 and 25 June 1999, OJ EPO 8–9/1999, pgs 545–553.
391. EPO OJ 1999, 545.
392. EPO OJ 2001, 549.
393. EPO- The London Agreement: European Patents and Cost of Translations; 2006.

(b) a state which does not have an official language in common with one of the official languages of the EPO shall dispense with the translation requirements provided for in Article 65(1) EPC if the European patent has been granted in the official language of the EPO prescribed by that state, or translated into that language and supplied under the conditions provided for in Article 65(1) EPC. These states may, however, require that a translation of the claims into one of their official languages be supplied;

(c) this agreement does not restrict the right of the state parties to this agreement to dispense with any translation requirement or to apply more liberal translation requirements than those previously referred;

(d) in case of dispute, the London Agreement does not restrict the right of the state parties to this agreement to prescribe that, in the case of a dispute relating to a European patent, the patent proprietor, at his own expense:
   - shall supply, at the request of an alleged infringer, a full translation into an official language of the state in which the alleged infringement took place;
   - shall supply, at the request of the competent court or quasi-judicial authority in the course of legal proceedings, a full translation into an official language of the state concerned.

770. The London Agreement entered into force on 1 May 2008, following the deposit of the instruments of ratification and accession by thirteen EPC Contracting States – including the three where the most European patents took effect in 1999, that is, France, Germany and the UK.[394] The following accessions after that date took effect [395] on the first day of the fourth month after the deposit of the instrument of accession.

771. The complete list of states members of the London Protocol and the day when started its effect for that state is as follows: Croatia, Denmark, France, Germany, Iceland, Liechtenstein, Latvia, Luxembourg, Monaco, Netherlands, Slovenia, Sweden, Switzerland, UK (1 May 2008); Albania (1 September 2013); Finland. Hungary (1 November 2011); Ireland (1 March 2014); Lithuania (1 May 2009); Former Yugoslav Republic of Macedonia (1 February 2012); Norway (1 January 2015).

772. It means that twenty-one Contracting States have ratified the London Agreement and correspondingly they dispensed, entirely or partly with the translation requirements under Article 65(1) EPC

773. A summary of the translation requirements in the Contracting States[396] could better clarify the impact of the London Protocol on translation costs of the European patents

---

394. London Agreement Art. 6(1).
395. London Agreement Art. 6(2).
396. EPO- National Law relating to EPC; Ch. IV. Translation Requirements After Grant.

774. Of the thirty-eight Contracting States to the EPC (status: 1 January 2018), seventeen of them, namely: Austria, Belgium, Bulgaria, Cyprus, the Czech Republic, Estonia, Greece, Italy, Malta, Poland, Portugal, Romania, San Marino, Serbia, Slovakia, Spain, and Turkey, have enacted provisions under Article 65 (1) and (2) EPC, subject to the condition that they are requiring the full translation of the patent specification.

775. Among them, eight Contracting States to the London Agreement, namely: France, Germany, Ireland, Liechtenstein, Luxembourg, Monaco, Switzerland, and the UK dispense entirely with the translation requirements due to the fact that they have at least one official language in common with the EPO that is.

776. Other remaining states, namely: Albania, Croatia, Denmark, Finland, Hungary, Iceland, the Netherlands, Norway, and Sweden do not have an official language in common with the EPO and require a translation of the claims to be filed in one of their official languages if the European patent has been granted in English or has been translated into English and filed under Article 65(1) EPC.

777. In these countries, except for Croatia, the European patent specification can also be filed in their national language.

778. The former Yugoslav Republic of Macedonia, Latvia, Lithuania, and Slovenia only require a translation of the claims into their respective official languages, regardless of the official language in which the EPO has granted the patent.

779. it is to be noted that all EPC Contracting States have provided in their national law, according to specific circumstances, that in accordance with Article 65(3) EPC, the failure to observe the relevant national provisions lead to the legal situation that the European patent will be deemed to be void *ab initio*.

Majority of laws of Contracting States provide also a non-extendable time limit for filing the translation.

§4. Relation with the Unitary Patent System

I. Legal Basis

780. As presented in Chapter 3 §10 I, in accordance with Article 142 of Part IX of the EPC, a group of Contracting States to the EPC may provide that the European patents granted for those states have a unitary character.

781. However, the effective creation of uniform patent protection throughout the EU is considered to originate in Article 118 of the Treaty on the Functioning of the European Union[397] (TFEU), among the measures to be taken in the context of the establishment and functioning of the internal market.

397. Official Journal of the European Union; C 115, Volume 51, 8 May 2008.

782. On 10 March 2011, the council adopted Decision 2011/167/EU of 10 March 2011 [398] authorizing enhanced cooperation between Belgium, Bulgaria, the Czech Republic, Denmark, Germany, Estonia, Ireland, Greece, France, Cyprus, Latvia, Lithuania, Luxembourg, Hungary, Malta, the Netherlands, Austria, Poland, Portugal, Romania, Slovenia, Slovakia, Finland, Sweden, and the UK (hereinafter 'participating Member States') in the area of the creation of UPP.

783. Based on that decision, Regulation (EU) No. 1257/2012 of the European Parliament and of the council of 17 December 2012 implementing enhanced cooperation in the area of the creation of UPP[399] and Council Regulation (EU) No. 1260/2012 of 17 December 2012 implementing enhanced cooperation in the area of the creation of UPP with regard to the applicable translation arrangements[400] which together provide the legal framework for the Unitary Patent system have been negotiated and adopted.

784. Regulation 1257/2012 constitutes a special agreement within the meaning of Article 142 of the EPC, a regional patent treaty within the meaning of Article 45(1) of the PCT of 19 June 1970 as last modified on 3 February 2001 and a special agreement within the meaning of Article 19 of the convention for the Protection of Industrial Property, signed in Paris on 20 March 1883 and last amended on 28 September 1979.

II. Select Committee and Secondary Legislation

785. After the adoption of these regulations, the participating Member States set up a Select Committee of the AC, in accordance with Article 145 EPC.

786. The committee has been set up by the twenty-five Member States that initially participated in the unitary patent to supervise the EPO's activities related to the tasks entrusted to it in the context of UPP. The committee's competencies include the setting of fees.

787. The committee held its inaugural meeting in Munich on 20 March 2013. Since then, it has adopted rules of procedure, a communication policy and a timeline for its work.

788. The committee is composed of a Chairman, Deputy Chairman, secretary, the participating Member States,[401] the EPO and observers, wherein this group are to be mentioned EC, EPI and BusinessEurope as well as representatives of the EPC Member States which are not participating in the Unitary Patent system.

---

398. OJ L 76, 22.3.2011.
399. OJ EPO 2013.
400. OJ EPO 2013.
401. As defined in Art. 2(a) of the Regulation No 1257/2012.

789. Starting in 2013, the Select Committee adopted the necessary secondary implementing legislation expressed as rules defining both internal working mechanism as well as the mechanism of the Unitary Patent system itself, namely:

- Rules relating to UPP,[402] providing for the establishment of a Unitary Patent Division at the EPO;
- Rules of Procedure of the Select Committee of the AC;
- Rules relating to Fees for UPP;[403]
- Budgetary and Financial Rules.[404]

790. Mentioned rules are incorporating and extending relevant EPC articles dedicated to unitary patent.

III. Main Characteristics of the Unitary Patent Protection

791. The future Unitary Patent is meant to be a 'European patent with unitary effect', which means a European patent granted by the EPO under the rules and procedures of the EPC to which, after grant, unitary effect is attributed for the territory of the EU Member States participating in the Unitary Patent scheme. After the grant of the European patent – but no later than one month after the mention of the grant is published in the European Patent Bulletin – the patent proprietor will have the new option to file a request for unitary effect with the EPO if he/she wishes to obtain a Unitary Patent. Based on the provisions of the EU Regulation No 1257/2012 on the Unitary Patent system, the EPO will be entrusted among other official tasks to perform[405]:

- receiving and examining requests for unitary effect;
- registering unitary effect;
- publishing translations during the transitional period;
- setting up and maintaining a new 'Register for Unitary Patent protection' containing entries
- on transfer, licensing, lapse, limitation or revocation of Unitary Patents;
- collecting annual renewal fees for Unitary Patents;
- distributing a share of the annual renewal fees to the participating Member States;
- administering a compensation scheme to support certain applicants, in particular SMEs, universities and public research organisations having their residence or principal place of business in an EU Member State, with a lump sum of EUR 500 to cover their translation costs if their European patent application leading to the Unitary Patent was filed in an official EU language other than English, French or German.

402. OJ EPO 2016.
403. OJ EPO 2016.
404. OJ EPO 2016.
405. EPO FAQ on the Unitary Patent; http://www.epo.org/law-practice/unitary/unitary-patent/faq.html.

792. Unitary Patents will make it possible to get patent protection in up to twenty-six EU Member States by submitting a single request to the EPO. They will build on European patents granted by the EPO under the rules of the EPC, so nothing will change in the pre-grant phase and the same high standards of quality search and examination will apply. After a European patent is granted, the patent proprietor will be able to request unitary effect, thereby getting a Unitary Patent which provides uniform patent protection in up to twenty-six EU Member States.

793. The Unitary Patent system practically means a new route of protection by which an inventor can protect an invention in Europe, outside national way or classical European patent way.

794. Comparing with classical granted European patents which must be validated and maintained individually in each country where they take effect, which is a complex and costly process, the unitary patent should offer a clear cost reduction. Unitary Patents should remove the need for complex and costly national validation procedures[406] and as a whole, they would in principle offer a series of advantages:

- The EPO acts as a one-stop-shop, allowing for a simple registration of a Unitary Patent.
- No fees are due for the filing and examination of the request for unitary effect or for registration of a Unitary Patent.
- No post-grant translations will be required after a six-year transitional period. During this period, a translation will be required for information only and will not have any legal effect.
- For EU-based SMEs, natural persons, non-profit organizations, universities and public research organizations a new compensation scheme will cover costs related to the translation of the patent application if it was filed in an official EU language other than English, French, or German. They will be paid a lump sum of EUR 500 when their Unitary Patent is registered.
- Unitary Patents will also not be subject to the currently fragmented fee renewal system: there will be only one procedure, currency, and deadline and no obligation to use a representative.
- The renewal fees have been set at a very competitive level and are particularly attractive for the first ten years, the average lifetime of a European patent. But applicants will also save on indirect costs. The more countries in which the European patent would have been validated, the greater the savings.
- All post-grant administration will be handled centrally by the EPO, further reducing costs and the administrative workload.
- The online register will include legal status information relating to Unitary Patents – notably on licences and transfers. This will also help to foster technology transfer and investment in innovation.

406. EPO- Unitary Patent; https://www.epo.org/law-practice/unitary/unitary-patent.html.

– Unitary Patents will confer truly uniform protection since the substantive patent law governing the scope and any limitations of the rights and the remedies available in cases of infringement has been harmonized in the agreement on a Unified Patent Court (UPCtA).

IV. Unified Patent Court

A. *Jurisdiction and Structure*

795. The Unitary Patent will become available when the UPCtA enters into force, meaning that thirteen Member States, including France, Germany and the UK must ratify this agreement.

796. The agreement establishes the Unified Patent Court (UPC) as a court of the Member States established by intergovernmental treaty between the participating states outside the framework of the EU but open only to members of the EU.

797. The UPC Agreement creates a specialized patent court with exclusive jurisdiction for litigation relating to Unitary Patents and European patents and aiming at harmonizing the scope and limitations of the rights conferred by a patent, and remedies available beyond EU Directive 2004/48/EC (Enforcement Directive).

798. The court will hear cases regarding infringement and revocation proceedings of European patents (including unitary patents) valid in the territories of the participating states, with a single court ruling being directly applicable throughout those territories.

799. The UPC will consist of a Court of First Instance (CFI), a Court of Appeal where can be appealed the decisions of the CFI, and a Registry.

800. The CFI will be one court with a central division and local and regional divisions. The central division will be located in Paris, with sections in London and Munich dealing with cases concerning specific patent classifications, wherefrom in London for human necessities, chemistry, and metallurgy, and in Munich for mechanical engineering, lighting, heating, weapons, and blasting.

801. Depending on the patenting activity, every Contracting Member State may request the UPC to set up, as part of the UPC CFI, up to four local divisions or a regional division together with one or more Contracting Member States.

802. The Court of Appeal will have its seat in Luxembourg where will also be the seat of the Registry. The panels of the Court of Appeal will operate under the Rules of Procedure of the UPC and will be based on a multinational composition. The language of proceedings before the Court of Appeal will be the language of proceedings before the CFI.

803. The Rules of Procedure for the UPC have been drafted and adopted in 2017 by the Preparatory Committee set up in 2013 by the twenty-five Member States who signed the agreement and who make up the membership of the Preparatory Committee.

804. Together with the UPC Agreement, Contracting Member States have adopted a declaration concerning the preparation for the coming into operation of the UPC and entrusted the Preparatory Committee of the UPC to prepare the practical arrangements and setting out a roadmap for the establishment and coming into operation of the new institution.

B. Competence[407]

805. Actions for or relating to infringement, provisional and protective measures and injunctions, damages, or compensation derived from provisional protection and/or prior use shall be brought before the local/regional division where the infringement has occurred, or at the choice of the plaintiff, where the infringer has residence or place of business. If the alleged infringement has occurred in the territories of several local or regional divisions of the CFI, the plaintiff has the possibility to choose between different divisions relating to the place of infringement. If the defendant has no residence or place of business in one of the Contracting Member States, actions shall be brought before the local/regional division where the infringement has occurred or before the central division. If the concerned Contracting Member State has no local/regional division, actions must be brought before the central division.

806. Actions for revocation or non-infringement must be brought before the central division unless an action for infringement between the same parties referring to the same patent has been already brought before a local or regional division, in case when these actions are to be brought before the same local/regional division.

807. Actions concerning decisions of the EPO, when carrying out administrative tasks regarding the UPP, must be brought before the central division.

808. If an infringement action is initiated before a local or regional division of the CFI and a counterclaim for revocation of the patent is brought before the local or regional division concerned, the local or regional division concerned may decide to proceed both with the infringement action and the counterclaim for revocation together;

809. It may alternatively decide to refer the counterclaim for revocation for the decision to the central division and depending on the circumstances of the case, either suspend or proceed with the infringement action.

---

407. EPO- An Enhanced European Patent System; The Select Committee, The Preparatory Committee; ttps://www.unified-patent-court.org/sites/default/files/enhanced-european-patent-system.pdf.

810. Subject to the agreement of the parties, the local or regional division concerned may also decide to refer both the infringement action and the counterclaim for revocation to the central division where they will be dealt with together.

811. Normally, after potential entering into function, the UPC should:[408]

- establish an effective forum for enforcing and challenging patents in Europe;
- end the need for litigation in different countries;
- enhance legal certainty through harmonized case law in the area of patent infringement and validity;
- provide simpler, quicker and more efficient judicial procedures;
- harmonize substantive patent law relating to the scope and limitations of the rights conferred as well as the remedies in cases of infringement.

C. *Sources of Law*

812. Article 24 of the agreement provides for the sources of law that judges should base their decisions on:

- Union law, including the two regulations regarding the unitary patent;
- Agreement on a UPC;
- The EPC;
- Other international agreements applicable to patents and binding on all the Member States;
- National law.

813. For the evaluation of which national law applies, regulations governing private international law – among others the Rome I and Rome II regulations – as part of the law of the EU as well as multilateral agreements are leading.

814. The decisions of the Court of Justice of the European Union (CJEU) are binding to the court.

§5. Relation with the EPLA (Draft)

815. Although not entered into force and having reduced chances to be entered in the future, an important reason for presenting the basis of EPLA was the fact that it represents an important legal achievement of the EPOrg in its effort to integrate in the European patent system, a true European litigation agreement able to deal in a synergic manner with the enforcement part of the system.

408. EPO- Unified Patent Court; https://www.epo.org/law-practice/unitary/upc.html#tab1.

816. The main reason for which EPLA has been practically left aside was the intended functioning of a UPC, as provided by the Unitary Patent system (*see* section §3 above).

817. It became more and more clear that once the process to build up the Unitary Patent system was advancing, a parallel building up of two different European litigation systems was difficult to accept.

818. The future of the Unitary Patent system, including that of the UPC as a counterpart for EPLA, is indeed a sensitive question, however, it is clear that the solid and harmonized legal and administrative bases that can be found in the construction of EPLA, might still offer future solutions for litigations at European level.

819. Based on a similar approach as those of the London Agreement, is to ne noted that the basis of the EPLA can be found when at an intergovernmental conference held in Paris in June 1999, the Member States of the EPOrg set up a Working Party on Litigation with the mandate[409] to submit to the Member States an optional agreement on an integrated judicial system for the settlement of litigation concerning European patents, The mandate was renewed at an intergovernmental conference held in London (October 2000), and after several years of intensive work in the Working Party on Litigation the draft of EPLA has been concluded.

820. The Working Party agreed to work on two basic legal instruments establishing the jurisdictional arrangements, namely:

– (Draft) Agreement on the establishment of a European patent litigation system.
– (Draft) Statute of the European Patent Court.

821. In September 2005, the sub-group of the Working Party on Litigation met to implement[410] into the draft Agreement on the establishment of a European patent litigation system the relevant provisions of Directive 2004/48/EC on the enforcement of intellectual Property Rights (IPR). The latest draft was submitted to the Working Party on Litigation for information on the occasion of its meeting on 14 December 2005, and thereafter the work of the Working Party was stopped.

822. EPLA provides for a common European Patent Court with jurisdiction to deal with infringement and revocation actions concerning European patents and provides also the setting up of a European Patent Court of Appeal, acting as Facultative Advisory Council, which is entrusted to deliver, upon request, non-binding opinions on the points of law concerning European or harmonized national patent law to national courts, with regard to infringement and validity actions.

409. EPO- Assessment of the impact of the European Patent Litigation Agreement (EPLA) on litigation of European patents; 2006.
410. EPO EPLA - European Patent Litigation Agreement; http://legaltexts.arcdev.hu/law-practice/legislative-initiatives/epla.html.

823. EPLA is an optional agreement according to which the EPC Contracting States can decide on their participation in the proposed integrated judicial system and if a state decides to participate, it has to opt between transferring jurisdiction to the European Patent Court or only allowing its courts to request for opinions to the Facultative Advisory Council.

824. The main characteristics of the draft EPLA are the following:

> The EPLA is an international agreement setting up a new European Patent Judiciary comprising a supervisory body – Administrative Committee – and the European Patent Court – Court of First Instance, Court of Appeal, and Registry – with jurisdiction over infringement and revocation actions concerning European patents;
>
> The Administrative Committee is made by representatives of the participating states, with the task to supervise the European Patent Court, without prejudice to the Court's judicial independence. It will also set up Regional Divisions upon request, appoint the judges and the Registrar and exercise important legislative and budgetary powers;
>
> The Court of First Instance is intended to comprise a Central Division and Regional Divisions located in some participating states. The common Court of Appeal will hear appeals against decisions of the Court of First Instance, and also act as Facultative Advisory Council, with the task of delivering, on request, non-binding opinions on any point of law concerning European or harmonized national patent law to national courts trying infringement and validity actions;

825. For both the first and second instance, international panels composed by legally and technically qualified judges will deal with cases in accordance with uniform rules of procedure including extensive powers for the court to order measures and impose securities, sanctions, and fines and to order provisional and protective measures. Panels are composed of three or five judges so that at least one judge shall be a technically qualified judge and at least two shall be legally qualified judges and the legally qualified judges shall be of at least two different nationalities.

826. Finally, national courts retain jurisdiction to order provisional or protective measures provided for by their national law and to order provisional seizure of goods as security for any damages, compensation, costs, or any other payment resulting from proceedings before the European Patent Court.

827. Substantive patent law contained in the agreement is based on the provisions of the 1989 Agreement relating to Community patents in defining direct and indirect infringement, limitation of the effects of the European patent, and the reversal of the burden of proof.

828. EPLA Agreement provides the application of Community law particularly, the Brussels and Lugano Conventions and Council Regulation 44/2001 and the possibility for the European Court of Justice in Luxembourg to issue, at request, preliminary rulings binding for the European Patent Court in so far as its decision takes effect in a Member State of the EU (MS).

829. The language regime is practically that of the EPC, adapted to post-grant litigation.

830. At first instance, the language of the proceedings will be before:

- the central division, the language of the proceedings before the EPO;
- a regional division located in a state having an EPO official language as official language, that official language;
- a regional division located in a state having either more than one or no official language which is one of the official languages of the EPO, any official language of the EPO designated by that state;
- the Court of Appeal, the language of the proceedings will always be the language of the first-instance proceedings.

831. With the agreement of the parties, the court may allow the use of a language other than the language of the proceedings during all or part of the proceedings.

Chapter 6. State of the Play and Predictable Evolution of the EPC

832. There are some key points which in our opinion might pave – on various scales and timing – a predictable future of the EPC, and they can be summarized as follows:

- political developments on the Unitary Patent system and specifically on the UPC;
- international developments in the field of patents;
- challenges to the future;
- internal evolution and needs of an improved procedure of the EPC

which will be shortly detailed in the following.

§1. Political Developments on the Unitary Patent System and Specifically on the UPC

833. Discussion under this topic starts from the fact that the EU regulations establishing the Unitary Patent system (No. 1257/2012 and No. 1260/2012) which entered into force on 20 January 2013, will only apply as from the date of entry into force of the UPC Agreement, that is, on the first day of the fourth month following the deposit of the thirteenth instrument of ratification or accession (provided those of France, Germany, and the UK).

834. As a matter of fact, by the date of publishing of this monograph, there are still pending problems arising from two of the relevant ratifying states namely, UK and Germany.

835. The process of UK ratification which the UK Government committed to in November 2015 is currently under a question mark and has clearly been slowed down since the UK voted on BREXIT to leave the EU in June 2016

836. The UPC Agreement currently requires participating countries to be EU members and two questions need appropriate answers in order to forecast a possible entry into force of the Unitary Patent system. Having in mind that BREXIT is scheduled to depart on Friday, 29 March 2019, the first question would be whether the UK would be able to participate in the new system if it does not ratify prior to that date;, the second one would be indeed whether, even if ratification takes place prior to the date the UK formally exits the EU, it will able to continue to participate in the regime of the new patent system post-BREXIT.

837. Another sensitive problem subsequently emerged in Germany where although earlier in 2017, the Parliament voted to ratify the UPC Agreement, however, due to an action brought in front of Germany's Constitutional Court, for the time, it is considering whether the legislation was constitutional.

838. Because our intention is to present possible political evolutions and not to comment on them, we will simply mention that it is largely considered that[411] 'the most likely scenario for the unitary patent and UPC system to survive the current challenges is for UK ratification to take place prior to 29 March 2019 and for the German constitutional complaint to be rejected by the Karlsruhe court in time for Germany to ratify prior to that date too'.

§2. International Developments in the Field of Patents

839. Under this topic, one could be envisaged three main areas of investigation for possible implications for the future of the EPC, namely:

- European level.
- WIPO level.
- Regional level.

840. Is rather obvious that the possible short and midterm evolutions at European level are entirely focused on the Unitary Patent system as we just analysed.

841. Regarding the second area, it starts from the point where, the necessity of a patent law internationally harmonized on substantive matters seemed almost obvious by the time EPC 2000 was signed, which led the international community to initiate the work on harmonization of substantive patent law at WIPO with a view to concluding a Substantive Patent Law Treaty (SPLT).

842. An agreement was made to deal with issues of direct relevance to the substantive patent law, in particular, the definition of novelty as relating to prior art, inventive step/non-obviousness, industrial applicability/utility, the drafting and interpretation of claims, and the requirement of sufficient disclosure of the invention and the 'grace-period'.

843. The topics – if agreed – could indeed lead to the necessity of having possible relevant points of the EPC revised and therefore the EPO took active part in the debates and negotiations. However, strong difficulties in finding common points of views among various groups of countries led to (the still existing situation) the SPLT negotiations being put on hold in 2006.[412]

844. A forecast on a possible evolution of SPLT seems unrealistic but if resumed, the EPC might involve significant amending points coming from an eventual internationally recognized harmonization of substantive matters.

---

411. *Michael Schneider* - Unified Patent Court project at risk amidst uncertainties in the UK and Germany October 2017; https://www.out-law.com/en/articles/2017/october/.
412. WIPO- Draft Substantive Patent Law Treaty; http://www.wipo.int/patent-law/en/draft_splt.htm.

845. Under the above circumstances, the five IP offices (IP5)[413] cooperation that was initiated in 2007 to address the issue of improving the efficiency of the examination process for patents worldwide due to growing backlogs and rapidly increasing filings receives a particular importance.

846. The IP5 is the name given to a forum of the five largest IP offices in the world that was set up to improve the efficiency of the examination process for patents worldwide.

847. This cooperation is founded on the pragmatic situation of the participating offices together handling about 80% of the world's patent applications and 95% of all the work carried out under the PCT.

848. However, the IP5 cooperation has, in principle and at least up to now, a minimum influence of the substance of the EPC but more on administrative questions arising from its procedural implementation.

849. The extremely relevant influence and force of these biggest offices in the world are materialized in the analyses and appropriate answers to a series of problems like:[414]

- rapidly growing volumes of prior art, particularly from Asia;
- increasing complexity of patent applications, especially in Information Technology (IT) and biotechnology;
- growing patent examination workload;
- patent examination quality;
- awareness of the importance of IP in general and of patents in particular;
- improving their patent information offerings and provide transparency for all stakeholders.

850. Some of the most significant initiatives of the IP5 could be summarized as follows:[415]

- aligning patent classification systems;
- stepping up IT-related initiatives;
- improving efficiency and quality;
- harmonizing patent practice and procedures;
- maintaining an effective partnership with IP5 Industry;
- increasing transparency and stakeholder involvement.

---

413. Forum of the five largest intellectual property offices in the world: theEPO, the Japan Patent Office (JPO), the Korean Intellectual Property Office (KIPO), the State Intellectual Property Office of the People's Republic of China (SIPO).
414. Forum of the five largest intellectual property offices in the world: the EPO, the Japan Patent Office (JPO), the Korean Intellectual Property Office (KIPO), the State Intellectual Property Office of the People's Republic of China (SIPO).
415. EPO -Meeting the Challenges of the Global Patent System - Initiatives of the EPO and its IP5 partners; 2015.

851. A direct implication on the administrative and procedural aspects of the EPC has the so-called partnership with IP5 users,[416] implying:

- Technical harmonization
- Common Citation Document – CCD
- Global Dossier services (IP5 file wrapper access)
- Procedural harmonization
- Unity of invention
- Citation of prior art
- Sufficiency of disclosure/written description.

852. Two concepts need a more specific attention as being relatively new and outside common legal or technical language.

853. The CCD application is part of the technical harmonization at international level aimed at establishing an appropriate infrastructure to facilitate greater integration of the global patent system and provides[417] a single point access to citation data supplied by more than thirty Patent Offices.

854. It consolidates the prior art cited for the same invention by all participating offices to be viewed on a single page for the family members of a patent application.

855. The Global Dossier is[418] an online public service launched in June 2014 by IP5 aiming at offering an integrated access to the respective 'file wrappers' free of charge and with automatic machine translations to English.

856. The file wrapper, also called 'public file', contains documents including the search reports, office actions, and correspondence between the applicant and the Patent Office relating to a particular patent application providing thus, the file history of a patent application

§3. Internal Evolutions and Needs of an Improved Procedure of the EPC

857. It is currently under discussions and following a large user consultation, a significant new line of action within the EPC will be developed, namely, the possibility to postpone the start of substantive examination called as User Driven Early Certainty (UDEC), for a duration of three years and upon an applicant's request.

416. *Ibid.*
417. EPO Common Citation Document (CCD) 21 Jul. 2017 Version 2.0; http://ccd.fiveipoffices.org/CCD-2.1.6/.
418. EPO IP5 file wrapper https://www.fiveipoffices.org/activities/globaldossier/filewrapper.html.

858. Postponement would occur within six months from the (supplementary) European search or from entry into the EP-phase (where the EPO does not perform a supplementary search) and the presumption is that it will involve no supplementary fee for the third party.

859. It is based on an overall action of offering to the users of the European patent, an 'early certainty' on procedural aspects of patentability within the EPO and in this respect, 'the Office has fully accomplished Early Certainty from Search (ECfS) and is well on track to achieve its – Early Certainty from Examination (ECfE) and Early Certainty from Opposition (ECfO) – three targets by 2020'.[419]

860. According to the intended purpose, this procedural step should offer no disadvantages for competitors or the public.

861. Another point of reflection is that during the process of examination, a substantiated, non-anonymous third-party observation can be filed.

862. Listed among the EPO's strategic priorities[420] are: maintaining a strong focus on quality, improving efficiency and harmonizing the international patent system in close cooperation with other Patent Offices and the user community. The increased internal efficiency of the EPO granting activity is also oriented towards a fully end-to-end digitalized 'EPO 4.0 and making Extensible Markup Language (XML) the preferred filing route at the EPO'.[421] It is expected that these priorities might indeed lead to a direct impact on the EPC and its amendment.

§4. Challenges to the Future

863. In a relevant and impressive paper[422] developed in 2007 under the EPO auspices including officials representing EPOrg Member States, four scenarios were developed to seek how international and European patenting might evolve over a horizon of up to 2015.

864. They were called:

(i) Market rules scenario: specific to a world where business is the dominant driver; this scenario goes toward the consolidation of a successful system but which might collapse under its own weight. New forms of subject matter – inevitably including further types of services – would become patentable and more players would enter the system.

419. EPO- User Driven Early Certainty (UDEC); 2018.
420. EPO -Meeting the Challenges of the Global Patent System - Initiatives of the EPO and its IP5 partners; 2015.
421. B. Batistelli- Recent Developments at the European Patent Office FICPI 17th Open Forum, 26 Oct. 2017, Venice.
422. EPO- Scenarios for the Future; pg. 10–11; Munich 2007.

(ii) Whose game? Scenario: forecasted for a world where geopolitics is the dominant driver; according to this scenario the patent world would evolve rather as a result of changing geopolitical balances and competing ambitions. No substantive changes on patentability are forecasted, but rather on enforcement, development and technology transfer.
(iii) Trees of knowledge scenario: oriented toward a world where society is the dominant drive; like the second scenario, neither in this one are foreseeable substantive changes on patentability, but rather on the modes to ensure that in the patenting process, knowledge remains a common good by also acknowledging the legitimacy of reward for innovation.
(iv) Blue skies scenario: drafted for a world where technology is the dominant driver. Complex new innovative technologies are considered as the key points to solving systemic problems, such as climate change, biotechnology, Information Technology Communication (ITC) technology, recycling technology, diffusion of technology. According to this scenario, the patent system[423] 'responds to the speed, interdisciplinary, and complex nature of the new technologies by abandoning the one-size-fits-all model: the former patent regime still applies to classic technologies while the new ones use other forms of IP protection such as the license of rights. The patent system relies on technology, and new forms of knowledge search and classification emerge'.

865. Our perspective is that there are no reasons to consider that the proposed scenarios and conclusions of the mentioned study are still remarkable to current times in spite of its relative age.

866. From the point of view of the forecastable evolutions of the EPC, which represents indeed our area of interest, it seems reasonable to substantiate the impact of new emerging technologies, in particular, ITC and biotechnology.

867. For instance, quite recently, on a proposal of the EPO, the AC took the decision, entered into force on 1 July 2017, to amend[424] the Rules 27 and 28 EPC in order to exclude plants and animals exclusively obtained by an essentially biological breeding process from patentability. The proposal from the EPO followed a notice of the EC from November 2016 related to certain articles in the EU Directive on biotechnological inventions (98/44/EC) which clarified in essence that the intended purpose of the Directive was to exclude not only processes but also products obtained by such processes. It was considered that[425] 'The EPO's proposal adopted by its Administrative Council ... safeguards uniformity in harmonised European patent law. It contains an important precision to patenting practice at the EPO, providing more clarity and legal certainty for users of the European patent system.'

---

423. EPO- Scenarios for the Future; pg. 10–11; Munich 2007.
424. EPO- EPO Clarifies Practice in the Area of Plant and Animal Patents- 29 Jun. 2017; https://www.epo.org/news-issues/news/2017/20170629.html.
425. *Ibid.*

868. On the others side, due to incredible rapid changes in the computer and ICT related matters, the European approach on the so-called computer/software-implemented inventions might indicate interesting evolutions, going from pure patenting practices in the EPO up to the necessity of amending the EPC Regulations.

869. For instance, a closer look is given currently[426] to the patentability of cloud computing technologies.

870. Another area of possible significant evolution relies on the fact that expected future developments of the UPC will impact the CII.[427] It is considered that 'the new court system will have enormous influence both on patent applications and existing portfolios in its role as nullity court for unitary European patents and traditional European patents, the UPC has the last word on patent eligibility for CIIs. A new doctrine may come into effect which puts the whole patent system at risk if it is less patent-friendly. Proprietors do not know to what extent the UPC will confirm the current EPO practice on CII protection. As the UPC approach to patent eligibility of CIIs will be uncertain for quite a number of years, applicants may well consider returning to the national PTOs for patent protection of CIIs where they find an established examination practice and jurisdiction'.

871. Another key point deriving from this perspective is expressed as,[428] 'in the mid to long-term, the UPC system, if it comes into force, will likely affect European software and Internet companies to a greater degree than the rules for patentability of CI inventions. Because the UPC is a step towards a Europe-wide court system for patent enforcement, it is possible that its establishment will result in a perception that patents in Europe are of higher value than they are at this point in time'.

426. Alain Strowel;Sinan Utku- The Trends and Current Practices in the Area of Patentability of Computer Implemented Inventions Within the EU and the U.S.; FINAL REPORT A study prepared for the European Commission DG Communications Networks, Content & Technology 2016; pg. 32–37.
427. Jonathan Sage Innovation in the Digital Single Market The role of Patents; 2015.
428. Alain Strowel;Sinan Utku- The Trends and Current Practices in the Area of Patentability of Computer Implemented Inventions Within the EU and the U.S.; FINAL REPORT A study prepared for the European Commission DG Communications Networks, Content & Technology 2016; pg. 32–37.

Selected Bibliography

Aplin Tanya, Davis Jennifer Intellectual Property Law Text, Cases, and Materials, Second Edition Oxford University Press.

Bardehle Pagenberg Assessment of Inventive Step under the EPC, 2015.

Bardehle Pagenberg The Patentability of Software under the EPC, 2015.

Beier Friedrich-Karl, Haertel Kurt, Schricker Gerhard Europaisches Patentubereinkommen, Munchener Gemeinschaftskommentar, Carl Heymanns Verlag KG 1998.

Benckard Georg – Patentgesetz§Gebrauchsmustergesetz, C.H.Beck'sche Verlagsbuchhandlung, München, 1993.

Chandler William Patentability of computer implemented inventions (CIIs): state of play and developments Official Journal EPO, 2015.

Chavanne Albert, Burst J.J. – Droit de la propriété industrielle, Dalloz – Paris, 1998.

Chisum Donald Jacobs Michael – Understanding I.P. Law, Mattew Bender, 1992.

Closa Daniel, Beaucé Gaëtan Examination of Computer Implemented Inventions CII and Business Methods Applications, EPO 2012.

Derk Visser – The Annotatetd European Patent Convention, H.TEL Publisher 2013.

Dybdahl Lise – European patents; Carls Heymans Verlag KG 2001.

EPO Boards of Appeal and Enlarged Board of Appeal Case Law 2015/2016.

EPO CA/16/98 and CA/16/98 Add.1- Points for a revision of the European Patent Convention; 1998.

EPO CA/PV 81 - Minutes of the 81st Meeting of the Administrative Council Munich, 5–7 September 2000.

EPO Case Law of the Boards of Appeal (2016 edition).

EPO Examination at the EPO as PCT Authority November 2017 edition.

EPO Guide for applicants: How to get a European patent, July 2017 (17th edition).

EPO Guidelines for Examination in the European Patent Office, November 2017 edition.

EPO National law relating to the EPC 18th edition, October 2017.

EPO- Scenarios for the future; April 2007.

EPO- The London Agreement: European patents and the cost of translations; 2006.

European Parliament -Policy Department C: The European Patent Office State of Play; Brussels, 2015.

Fox Nicholas- A Guide to the EPC 2000; CIPA 2007.

Fritz Stephan, Grunbeck Elisabeth, Hijazi Ali- Schlussel zum europaisechen Patentubereinkommen 2001; Stampfli Verlag AG Bern 2002.

Selected Bibliography

Griset Pascal- The European Patent A European Success Story for Innovation; Käsel Buch 2013.

Krasser Rudolf- Lehrbuch des Patentrechts; C.H.Beck's Munchen; 4 Auflage 1986.

Mathely, Paul. *Le nouveau droit fracais des brevets des inventions*. JNA, 1991.

Nack Ralph, Phélip Bruno- AIPPI REPORTS -Report on the Diplomatic Conference for the Revision of the European Patent Convention.

Pagenberg Jochen Europaisches Patentubereinkommen, Munchener Gemeinschaftskommentar, Carl Heymanns Verlag KG 1995.

Paterson Gerald- The European Patent System- The Law and Practice of the European Patent Convention; Sweet & Maxwell 1992.

Pitkethly Robert- The European Patent System: Implementing Patent Law Harmonisation.

Seville Catherine- EU Intellectual Property Law and Policy; Elgar European Law; 2016 Second Edition.

Schulte, Reiner Patentgesetz mit EPU 9, neuarbeitete und erweiterteAuflage, Karl Heymans Verlag KG, 2007.

Stauder, Dieter, Margarete Singer – The European Patent Convention, Carl Heymanns Verlag KG 2003.

Stauder, Dieter, Margarete Singer. *EuropaischesPatentubereinkommen Kommentar*. Carl Heymans Verlag KG, 2000.

Straus Joseph – Deutsches und europaisches Patentrecht, Max Planck, 2001.

Strenc Alexandru – European Software Directives and European Software Patents. Wolters Kluwer 2017.

Strenc, Alexandru, Bucura Ionescu§ Gheorghe Gheorghiu. *Treaty on Patent Law*. Editura Lumina Lex, 2005 2007.

Strenc, Alexandru. Information Technology.Protection and Enforcement of Intellectual Property Rights.Editura Universul Juridic, Colectia Bussines 2010.

Strowel Alain, Utku Sinan- The Trends and Current Practices in the Area of Patentability of Computer Implemented Inventions Within the EU and the U.S.; A study prepared for the European Commission DG Communications Networks, Content & Technology; 2016.

Teschmacher Rudolph- Europaisches Patentubereinkommen, Munchener Gemeinschaftskommentar, Carl Heymanns Verlag KG.

Visser Derek- The Annotated European Patent Convention, 21st revised edition. H.TEL, Publisher 2013.

WIPO PCT / AAQ/IV- Report on the Results of the Munich Diplomatic Conference for the Setting up of a European System for the Grant of Patents; prepared by the International Bureau, 18 October 1973.

Index

The numbers here refer to paragraph numbers.

Abstract, 274, 430, 442
Accordance, 78, 474
Additional international search fee, 114
Administration of justice, 520, 549
Administrative and legal cooperation, 144
Administrative Council, 9, 171
Administrative fees, 253
Advances, 817
Agreement, 642
Agriculture, 363
Amending of, 106
Amendment, 4, 118
Animal varieties, 290–291
Animals, 290
Appeal, 113
Appeals procedure, 113, 547 et seq.
Applicants, 663–676
Application, 663–676
Assessment, 331–336
Author, 756
Authorization, 604, 726
Authority, 756–758

Board, 228–232
Board of Appeal, 566–579
Branch at The Hague, 124, 128–129, 168, 185, 187

Calculation, 321,
Categories, 372, 444, 445
Chairman, 230
Chairmanship, 227
CII, 356, 358
Claim, 313, 315
Claims fee, 48, 97–99, 315–318, 397
Clarity, 867
Classification, 33
Closest prior art, 339, 342, 344–348
Comments, 759
Commercial purpose, 360
Common provisions, 585–600
Communication, 121, 402, 451–453
Competence, *see* powers
Composition, 222–227
Computer implemented invention *see* CII
Computer program, 90–93
Computer software, 277, 355, 868
Computers, 276 et seq.
Condition of patentability, 260
Conference of ministers, 165
Confirmation, 290
Content, 147–152
Contract, 184, 420
Contracting States, 656–662
Contribution, 356–358
Conversion, 623–630
Cooperation, 235
Correction, 476
Costs, 118–120
Court, 795–804
Creation, 275
Criminal acts, 113, 572, 574

Date of filing, 78
Date of priority, 321, 333, 439, 458, 484, 628, 638,
Death or legal incapacity of the ~, 147 et seq.
Decision, 528 et seq., 553–559, 566–579
Deficiencies, 476
Definition, 303
Denunciation of the, 684
Departments of the EPO, 646–650
Dependent claims *see* claims
Deposit, 682, 770, 883
Deputy Chairperson, 201, 227

Index

Description, 48, 366, 370, 413–414, 449
Designated Office, 481, 497
Designation, 439
Diagnostic methods, 292–300
Different, 397
Directorate, 210
Directorates-General, 207, 211–214
Disclosure, 319–330
Discoveries, 272
Dispute, 687
Divisional application, 429
Document, 133–135
Documentation, 243
Drawings, 48, 414, 430, 434, 464, 481, 633
Duration, 329
Duties, 197–198

Elected Office, 676
Employees, 711
Employer, 377
Enlarged Board of Appeal, 203–204, 566–579
Entitled, 371–382
Entitlement, 523–527
Entry in the Register, 203
EPC, 23 et seq.
EPI, 611
EPOrg, 168 et seq.
Equivalence, 623, 626
EURO-PCT, 114–117, 749
European divisional application, 429
European patent, 1 et seq.
European patent application, 100–102, 383 et seq., 418 et seq., 422 et seq., 430 et seq.
European Patent Bulletin, 221, 390, 396, 460, 465, 482, 486, 493, 497, 528, 533, 536, 595, 641, 671, 674, 791
European Patent Convention *see* EPC
European Patent Office *see* EPO
European Patent Organisation *see* EPOrg
European patent specification, 399, 440, 501, 777
European patent with unitary effect, 791–794
European search report, 465, 468, 482, 505–506, 674
Evidence, 322
Examination, 474 et seq.
Exceptions, 292
Exceptions to patentability, 41, 281–300
Exchange of, 213
Excluded from patentability, 267 et seq.
Exclusive right, 268, 298
Expression, 525, 627
Extension, 9, 174–176, 178–180, 247–248, 387
Extent of, 103–105, 408–417

Failure to reply, 489
Feature, 280, 299–300
Fee, 253
Field of technology, 269
Filing, 81, 83, 134, 398–399, 422–429
Form, 442, 444
Formal requirements, 83, 129, 474, 629

Grant of a European patent, 379–380, 433, 439, 696–698
Grounds or evidence, 585
Group, 217, 644–655

Hague, 128–133
Health, 94–99
Human body, 281, 297–300, 317

Idea, 36, 274, 736
Identity, 284
Immunities, 706–712
Implementing Regulations, 20, 137–139, 689–695
Independent claims, 444–445
Industrial application, 362–370
Information, 280
Information Technology, 864
Infringement, 514
Institute of Professional Representatives *see* EPI
Instruments of accession and ratification, 682
Insufficient, 447
Intergovernmental organizations, 225
Interlocutory revision, 558
International, 16, 25, 33
International application, 663 et seq.
International exhibitions, 319, 323
International preliminary examination, 676, 757
International Preliminary Examining Authority, 666–668, 719–722
International search report, 674
Inventive step, 337 et seq.

Joint, 655

Joint applicants *see* applicants
Joint designation *see* designation
Joint proprietors *see* proprietor of the patent
Jurisdiction, 795–804

Lack of, 114
Language, 215–221
Lapse, 62, 383, 628
Legal Division, 203
Legal person, 168, 218
Legal provision, 364
Legislation, 785
Liability, 183–186
Licence, 420–421
Licensee, 514
List of professional representatives, 605, 607, 617
London, 761–779

Made availability to the public, 301, 302, 303, 402
Meetings, 30–33
Members, 172
Methods, 94 et seq., 272, 276
Methods for treatment, 292–300
Microbiological, 289
Mistakes *see* errors in documents
Morality, 282–284
Multiple, 458
Multiple applicants *see* applicants
Multiple inventors *see* inventor
Multiple priorities, 451, 458, 459
Multiple priorities *see* priority
Munich, 55 et seq., 69 et seq.

Name, 436, 589, 742, 846
National, 623–630
Natural person, 606
Non-prejudicial, 319–330
Notification, 557, 680
Novelty, 301 et seq.

Ordre public, 72, 282–284

Period of, 324
Periodical, 321
Person skilled in the art, 47, 351–359
Persons entitled, 371–382
Petition for review, 113, 473, 572, 575
Powers, 805
Prejudice, 333, 531
Premises, 187–190
Presentation, 280
Prior art, 100–102
Prior use, 329
Priority, 133
Priority date *see* date of priority
Priority right, 451, 453, 456
Privileges and immunities *see* immunities
Problem, 339–346
Problem and solution approach, 341
Procedure, 528–545
Proceedings, 110–112
Process, 546
Products, 387
Professional representatives *see* representatives
Programs for computers, 267, 277
Property, 418
Proprietor, 518
Proprietor of the patent, 390, 448, 518, 535, 586, 634, 761
Protection, 103–105, 383–388, 408–417
Protocol on the Interpretation, 728–741
opposition proceedings. 511–520
Provisional protection, 67, 400, 402–404, 672, 805
Public prior use *see* prior use
Publication, 72, 464–465, 481–482, 497

Receiving Office, 666, 676, 757
Receiving Section, 124, 129, 203, 474
Recognition, 696–700
Re-establishment of rights, 86, 139, 591, 592
Refund, 757
Refusal, 404, 439, 468, 476
Register of European Patents, 221
Reimbursement, 111
Rejection, 105
Renewal fees, 65, 253, 460, 640–641, 652
Representation, 601–622
Representatives, 224, 225, 227, 232, 611
Request, 107–108, 110–111, 485–487
Request for grant, 433, 436
Residence, 702
Restitutio in integrum *see* re-establishment of rights
Revocation, 631–635
Right, 636–638
Right to an EP, 376, 378, 438
Right to use, 596
Rights conferred by, 797

Rule, 203, 390, 402, 627
Rules of Procedure, 228, 240–243, 552

Scientific theories, 272–274
Scope of protection, 104, 107, 416, 733, 736
Search, 474
Search report, 115–116, 463, 477–478, 482, 505–506, 674
Searching Authority, 16, 114–116, 495, 666–668, 714, 716, 717, 719
Select Committee, 237, 647–648, 785–790
Signature, 34, 419
Software, 93, 277
Solution, 339–346
Specification, 498–500
  patentability, 263–271, 278–279, 281
Staff, 187–192, 742–743
State of the art, 301, 302–310
Structure of the EPO, 196 et seq., 795 et seq.
Subject matter, 18, 88, 263, 268
Sub-office, 185, 188–189
Subsequently, 21, 113, 464, 481
Substances and composition, 96
Substantive patent law, 88–105, 827, 841, 842
Surgery, 281, 294, 296–298

Taxation, 712
Taxes, 712
Technical, 235
Technical character, 263–264, 276
Technical effect, 273
Technical field, 352–356
Technical means, 272, 275, 279, 280
Technical opinion, 195
Technical problem, 264, 339–341, 343, 345, 347–348, 739–740
Terms of office, 735, 736
Territorial effect, 680, 798
The Hague *see* branch at The Hague, 124
Therapy, 99, 297, 299
Third parties, 329
Time limits, 139, 395, 428
Transfer, 137–138
Transfer of rights, 421
Translation, 389–397
Transmission, 628, 629
Transmittal, 629–630
Treaty, 148, 750 et seq.

Unreasonable prejudice, 319–330

Vienna, 188, 189
Voting rights, 250
Voting rules, 251

Weighting of votes, 250
Work, 229

www.ingramcontent.com/pod-product-compliance
Lightning Source LLC
Chambersburg PA
CBHW071342230926
51846CB00002B/419
9789403503042